Books by Sigurd F. Olson

THE LONELY LAND (1961)

LISTENING POINT (1958)

THE SINGING WILDERNESS (1956)

These are BORZOI BOOKS
published by ALFRED A. KNOPF *in New York*

THE LONELY LAND

Sigurd F. Olson

THE LONELY

Illustrations by Francis Lee Jaques

LAND

Alfred A. Knopf *1961* NEW YORK

L. C. catalog card number: 60–53233

THIS IS A BORZOI BOOK,
PUBLISHED BY ALFRED A. KNOPF, INC.

FIRST EDITION

To

the Voyageurs who have been with me

in the

Lonely Land

UNITED STATES AIR FORCE

ACKNOWLEDGMENTS

I AM DEEPLY GRATEFUL for criticism and encouragement by members of my family, particularly my son Sigurd, of Alaska, who suggested the title of this book, and to Ann Langen, whose patient and understanding participation in the typing and editing of successive revisions of the manuscript brought it finally to completion. To Marie Rodell, my agent, to Angus Cameron, my editor, and to Alfred A. Knopf go my thanks for suggestions and help.

Francis Lee Jaques has my sincere appreciation for the superb and powerful sketches of the North country.

I am indebted also to Dr. G. M. Schwartz and the Geology Department of the University of Minnesota for professional advice and counsel; to Eric Morse of Ottawa, who read the entire manuscript for historical and geographical accuracy; to Denis Coolican for permission to use his personal diary of the Churchill Expedition as a check against my own, and to the other voyageurs whose reactions I treasure.

I wish to thank Charles Scribner's Sons for permission to quote from *Green Hills of Africa* by Ernest Hemingway; Dr. Edmund W. Sinnot of Yale University for an excerpt from *My Faith*; *Maclean's Magazine* for permission to quote from "The Romance of the Canadian Shield" by Blair Fraser;

ACKNOWLEDGMENTS

the Minnesota Historical Society for excerpts from Dr. Grace Lee Nute's *The Voyageur* and *The Voyageur's Highway*.

My thanks go also to the Champlain Society of Toronto for permission to quote from the following historical records and diaries: Sir George Simpson's *Athabasca Journal*, edited by E. E. Rich, with an introduction by Chester Martin; David Thompson's *Narrative of Explorations in Western America 1784–1812*, edited by J. B. Tyrrell; *The Journals of Samuel Hearne and Philip Turnor*, edited by J. B. Tyrrell.

The following sources supplied invaluable information on the fur trade and life of the era:

The Moose Fort Journals of 1783–85, published by the Hudson's Bay Record Society of London; *A Journal of Voyages and Travels in the Interior of North America* by Daniel Harmon, published by Allerton Book Company of New York; *Travels through the Interior Parts of North America in the years 1766, 1767, 1768* by Jonathan Carver, printed in London by John Cookley Lettsom in 1781; Alexander Mackenzie's famous *Voyages from Montreal* (in the years 1789 and 1793), published by A. S. Barnes & Company of New York in 1903; *The Journals of Alexander Henry the Younger and of David Thompson 1799–1814*, published by Francis P. Harper in New York in 1897; and *La Salle* by Louise S. Hasbrouck, the Macmillan Company, New York, 1919.

I am grateful to Frank B. Hubachek, who made many of these volumes available to me at his historical library at the Wilderness Research Center on Basswood Lake, and to William Trygg, who also supplied me with reference works.

To the Hudson's Bay Company, without whose generous co-operation and enthusiastic help the Churchill Expedition might not have been possible, go my own personal thanks and that of the voyageurs who were with me.

CONTENTS

ix

CONTENTS

THE LONELY LAND

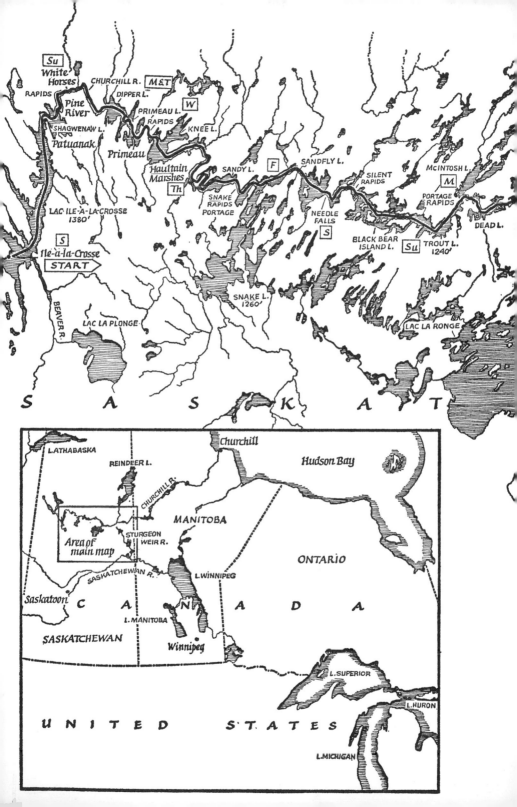

The
LONELY
LAND

map by palacios

Scale of miles

0   10   20   30   40   50

N

W   E

S

MANITOBA

SASKATCHEWAN

REINDEER R.

CHURCHILL R.

CHURCHILL R.

L RAPIDS

OTTER RAPIDS

T OTTER L.

FALLS

MOUNTAIN L.

Stanley Mission

W NISTOWIAK L.

F
TRADE L.

FALLS

KEG L.

Th
ISKWATIKAN L.

KEG FALLS

GRAND RAPIDS

FROG PORTAGE

MANAWAN L.

RAPIDS

WOOD L.

S

PELICAN L.

Pelican Narrows

Su

MIROND L.

CORNEILLE L.

Maligne

M

STURGEON WEIR R.

Flin Flon

AMISK L.

GOOSE L.

T

STURGEON WEIR R.

W
Sturgeon Landing

GOOSE R.

NAMEW L.

CUMBERLAND L.

Th

FINISH

Cumberland House

OLD CHANNEL

F

SASKATCHEWAN R.

TO THE PAS

THE LONELY LAND

THERE ARE few places left on the North American continent where men can still see the country as it was before Europeans came and know some of the challenges and freedoms of those who saw it first, but in the Canadian Northwest it can still be done. A thousand miles northwest of Lake Superior are great free rivers, lakes whose horizons disappear, countless unnamed waterways, and ridges and forested valleys still largely unknown. Most of it is part of the Canadian Shield, an enormous outpouring of granitic lava that extends from the bleak coasts of Labrador in the east, almost to the Mackenzie River valley in the west and then on into the Arctic North.

It is a vast and lonely land, for as yet only its southern fringes

5

have been occupied. The rest is neither settled nor pierced by roads. Though planes have mapped most of it and jets fly high above with vapor trails floating even over the tundras south of the Arctic coast, though a few mining camps serviced by air can be found far in the interior, few men know it well. Hudson's Bay Posts and installations of the Royal Canadian Mounted Police are scattered throughout it and at such locations are often found the missions of the Oblate Fathers of Montreal and the Anglican Church of Canada. There are Indian settlements, the Crees and Chippewyans, the Yellow Knives, the Dog Ribs, and Hares, along the great rivers that have always been their major routes of travel and migration, but the land itself has changed little since the days of the fur trade and exploration.

This was the region the French voyageurs explored and traveled after they knew the country between the St. Lawrence and the Great Lakes. Beyond Lake Superior until 1650, the Northwest was the vast unknown, perhaps the fabled passage to the Pacific, the greatest frontier of the new world. For two hundred years these intrepid canoemen probed its farthermost reaches trading wherever they went, establishing posts at strategic points, weaving a vast network of influence over the entire region. During those days fortunes in fur were carried across the portages and paddled down the waterways to satisfy the markets of the east. In the two or three thousand miles between Montreal and the far Northwest, these French Canadians lived and traveled with a spirit, sense of adventure and pride in their calling that balanced its enormous distances and hardships. These wiry little men—seldom more than five feet four or five—dressed in breech cloth, moccasins and leather leggings reaching to thighs, a belted shirt with its inevitable colored pouch for tobacco and a pipe, topped off with a red cap and feather. They were a breed apart. From dawn until dark they paddled their great canoes and packed enormous loads, facing storms, wild uncharted rivers, hostile Indians and ruthless rivals with a joy and abandon that has possibly never been equaled in man's conquest and exploitation of any new country.

Each spring at the breakup of ice on the St. Lawrence, great brigades of canoes left Montreal for the west, hundreds of gay and colorful craft fashioned from birchbark, cedar, and spruce. There were the huge thirty-five foot Montreals with a crew of fourteen, the Bastard Canoes with a crew of ten, the twenty-five foot North Canoes and the Half Canoes, for such inland waters as those beyond Grand Portage. Decorated in gaudy designs, each brigade with its own insignia, vermilion-tipped paddles moving in rhythm to the chansons of Old France, here was a pageant such as the New World had never known and will never see again.

In command of each brigade was the Bourgeois whose word was law. It was he who decided when to start and stop and where to go. In his charge was the precious cargo of trade goods and the responsibility of converting it into fur. These men were usually of Scotch or English origin—Mackenzies, McGillivrays, McTavishes, Simpsons, and McLeods. To them this country and its vast resources were there to be exploited.

While they left voluminous diaries and meticulous journals, there is little in them of appreciation of the life they led. To them the country meant fur and fur meant profit. Indians were the means of acquiring it and the voyageurs merely a source of power for the sole purpose of transporting trade goods into the interior and furs back either to Montreal on the St. Lawrence or to York Factory on Hudson Bay. With the exception of a few men such as Peter Pond, Samuel Hearne, or David Thompson, they were seldom impressed with the stark beauty or romance of the land they traversed. To them the fur trade was a business proposition and if at the end of a season the books balanced with a profit, that was all that mattered. Still, without the shrewdness, indomitable will, and vision of these men—the partners and clerks of the various companies, the free traders, and the Bourgeois of the brigades—this commerce would not have developed on the continental scale that it did.

Thousands of men were in the trade from the early sixteen hundreds until approximately a hundred years ago. The routes they traveled were as familiar to them as our transcontinental highways are to us. Nothing was thought of leaving Montreal or the Bay for such distant points as Grand Portage on Lake Superior, Cumberland House in the Saskatchewan country, or Fort Chippewyan at the end of Lake Athabasca. A few thousand miles of travel by canoe was as accepted a procedure in those days as taking an automobile trip today.

For a century and a half the French were in control, but after 1760 and the conquest of Canada by the British, the ancient emblem of France, the Fleur-de-lis, was seen no more in the far country. Grace Lee Nute says:

"Kings came and went, governments rose and fell, wars were fought and boundary lines placed at will, but the border country cared little. Its life went on as before, full of activity, danger, adventure, the struggle of existence, the round of ordinary life in a region that was virtually a law unto itself."

The last century of the trade was a time of fierce competition and the men of the various companies, particularly the North West and Hudson's Bay companies, as well as the free traders, fought bitterly for fur. While it is true the voyageurs sang as they paddled their canoes and made merry with the Indians at the encampments, they also fought pitched battles with their enemies, ambushed rivals and stole their supplies and fur. It was a common practice to intercept bands of Indians taking fur to rival posts, fur that had already been paid for by others. Nothing was thought of piracy or of debauching the Indians with rum to make them amenable. There was bloodshed on lakes and portages, and camp sites. Murder went unpunished for there was no law that extended into the hinterlands. The gathering of fur was a deadly serious business to everyone except the voyageurs themselves.

George Simpson of the Hudson's Bay Company must have been very conscious of this as he worked his way up the Churchill in 1820.

"Embarked at half past three AM; passed Fourteen N.W. Canoes. I could not help remarking with much concern the striking contrast between our Brigade and that of our Opponents; all their Canoes are new and well built of good materials, ably manned, a water proof arm chest and casette for fineries in each, and the baggage covered with new oil cloths, in short well equipped in every respect: on the other hand, our Canoes are old, crazy, and patched up, built originally of bad materials without symmetry and neither adapted for stowage nor expedition; manned chiefly by old infirm creatures or Porkeaters unfit for the arduous duty they have to perform. . . . At four O'Clock observed a half loaded Canoe pushing across the River towards us, it turned out to be Simon McGillivray who merely came alongside to make his observations; This Gentleman I understand has been most active in every nefarious transaction that has taken place in Athabasca, he is notorious for his low cunning, has made Mr. Clarke a prisoner twice and threatens to have him soon again . . . next to Black he is more to be dreaded than any member of the N.W. Coy.; he was the principal leader of the lawless assemblage of Halfbreeds and Indian assassins at the Grand Rapid this season; a day of retribution I trust is at hand for this worthy."

With the absorption of the North West Company and other rivals by the Hudson's Bay Company in 1821, competition came to an end. Gradually the trade declined, due partly to the settlement of the west, changing fashions in fur, and because many parts of the country had been exhausted by heavy trapping and hunting. While the Hudson's Bay Company still has far-flung outposts, the old days are gone forever.

All that is left of those colorful days of the past are crumbling forts, old foundations, and the names the voyageurs gave to lakes and rivers and portages. But there is something that will never be lost; the voyageur as a symbol of a way of life—the gay spirit with which he traveled, his singing as he paddled his canoe, and a love of the wilderness that practically depopulated the struggling pioneer settlements along the St. Lawrence during the heyday of the trade.

Grace Lee Nute in her book *The Voyageur* sums up the feeling of them all in one trenchant paragraph from an old journal:

"Said one of these men, long past seventy years of age: 'I could carry, paddle, walk and sing with any man I ever saw. I have been twenty four years a canoe man, and forty one years in the service; no portage was ever too long for me. Fifty songs could I sing. I have saved the lives of ten voyageurs. Have had twelve wives and six running dogs. I spent all my money in pleasure. Were I young again, I should spend my life the same way over. There is no life so happy as a voyageur's life.'"

Ghosts of those days stalk the portages and phantom brigades move down the waterways, and it is said that singing still can be heard on quiet nights. I wonder when the final impact of the era is weighed on the scales of time if the voyageur himself will not be remembered longer than anything else. He left a heritage of the spirit that will fire the imaginations of men for centuries to come.

For a long time I dreamed of the Northwest, of exploring it by canoe as I had explored the lake country of the Quetico-

Superior. The beautiful waterways I had come to know so well along the Minnesota-Ontario border seemed the answer to my own need of wilderness and my interest in the voyageurs until the summer I made an expedition with a group of Canadian friends along the old La Vérendrye route from Grand Portage on Lake Superior to Fort Francis almost three hundred miles away. Along that route something happened to us that made us determined to follow the ancient trail we had begun far into the Northwest.

The urge began the moment we pitched our tents near the rebuilt North West Company stockade on the north shore of Lake Superior. Gagnon's Island lay like a watchdog off the entrance to Grand Portage Bay. Hat Point with the gnarled old Witches Tree at its tip was waiting as always for the brigades to come by. In the blue distance was the shadowy outline of Isle Royale. It was the same as the day in 1731 when La Vérendrye and his voyageurs made the terrible nine-mile carry around the rapids of the Pigeon River toward the unknown country beyond for the first time. That night those men were with us and when the haze of our campfire drifted along the beach, it seemed to join with the smoke of long forgotten fires and lay like a wraith over the canoes, tepees, and tents along the shore.

When we broke camp the following morning and toiled up the Grand Portage to the top of the first plateau, they moved beside us. When we stopped to rest and looked back at the blue sparkling expanse of Lake Superior, we saw it through their eyes. That day we struggled through bogs and muskegs with them, fought our way over hills and rocks and ledges, suffered from black flies and mosquitoes, made the same poses or rests after each half mile, and dreamed of the moment we would glimpse blue water, drop our loads, and take to the canoes once more.

Though there were no shouts of welcome at the landing, voyageurs were still with us. All along the trail Vérendrye blazed was a consciousness of them and of the land to which the Quetico-Superior was but the gateway. More and more our thoughts became involved with them, until by the time the trip was over at the far end of Rainy Lake, we knew that within a year or two we must follow them into the Northwest.

The plan for our first expedition into the Lonely Land was born at a gathering of the veterans of the La Vérendrye route at Ottawa during the following winter. We met around a table spread with maps, pictures, and diaries and as we talked of Athabasca, Great Slave, and the Churchill River country, this hitherto nebulous land became real to us and its names began to have meaning. None of us had forgotten the previous summer and how the men of the old brigades had been with us. As we read from their diaries, the wild country they had explored became alive.

Somewhere in northwestern Saskatchewan, near the height of land between the waters flowing north into the Arctic and those flowing east into Hudson Bay, would be our starting point. We would travel downstream as though we had wintered there, beginning at the historic old post at Ile à la Crosse close to the headwaters of the Churchill River, follow it for five hundred miles across the top of the province and then southeast to Flin Flon or possibly Cumberland House. It was one of the most famous routes of all and so well traveled that during the days of the trade it was considered a major highway from the Mackenzie.

We chose it because it was the way the Athabasca brigades had come on their way to the Quetico-Superior to meet those from Montreal at Grand Portage. Nowhere in the Northwest could we find a route that had seen more of the life of that era. Every portage, every camp site, every mile of that great waterway was steeped in the annals of trade and exploration. Here if anywhere we might capture the feel of the old days.

It is a difficult thing to recapture the sense of any time that is gone, hard to realize the meaning of Daniel Boone's Wilderness Trail, the route of Lewis and Clark, or of Coronado, unless you can travel as those men did, see the terrain as they saw it, and live in the same primitive way. Only in a region of great unbroken distances where men can travel for weeks or months away from roads and towns can this be done. The Churchill River country was still relatively unchanged.

We had no idea of emulating the voyageurs or performing their feats. We had traveled enough together in the Quetico-Superior and other areas to know our limitations. We considered ourselves experienced on rivers and lakes and portages and knew what we could do as modern voyageurs. Our standard load for instance would seldom be more than a hundred pounds, while they never carried less than one hundred and eighty, and often more. Ours was the best of modern equipment, sixteen-foot Prospector canoes made by Peterborough instead of birchbarks, tents with mosquito netting, insect bombs and repellents, down sleeping bags instead of a shoddy blanket for each, air mattresses, waterproof rain gear and ponchos, the best of dehydrated foods, but more important than all else were our excellent maps.

We seldom got under way in the morning before six or seven and always made camp well before dark. They often started before dawn, paddled several hours before breakfast and continued until nine or ten o'clock at night. We would average twenty or thirty miles a day, while they often doubled and sometimes even tripled that distance, because they had more paddlers and were on the water from fourteen to sixteen or even eighteen hours a day. We would attempt no such heroic feats for we wanted to enjoy the wilderness and try to catch something of the drama of the era of which those men were a part.

We would paddle the same lakes, however, run the same rapids and pack over the same portages. We would know the wind and the storms and see the same sky lines, and because it was our first expedition into the far Northwest we might feel some of the awe and wonderment and even the fear and delight at the enormous expanses and the grandeur of a new land.

The quotations preceding each chapter and interspersed throughout are taken mostly from the diaries of a number of men who traveled the route between 1770 and 1870. Their records give us a sense of personal relationship that somehow bridges the gap between those days and the present. Although place names have changed many times since then—sometimes to English, French, or Cree—and most of the journals, particularly those of Alexander Mackenzie and George Simpson, were made coming upstream rather than downstream, they cover the general area of our experience and in all of them is the color and flavor of the country itself.

If a man can pack a heavy load across a portage, if he can do whatever he has to do without complaint and with good humor, it makes little difference what his background has been. And if he can somehow keep alive a spark of adventure and romance as the old-time voyageurs seem to have done, then any expedition becomes more than a journey through wild country. It becomes a shining challenge and an adventure of the spirit.

Without exception on all of the trips we have made, laughter has been the rule and in each case we have accomplished what we set out to do. Since the Churchill there have been others: the God's Lake–Hayes River route toward Hudson Bay, the Reindeer-Athabasca, Methye Portage and the Clearwater, the Camsell River from Great Slave to Great Bear, and the Mackenzie. On those I have been privileged to make, my companions have been men who not only did what was expected of them but who also contributed some unique and special quality that made each venture a memorable one. With me on the Churchill were men who had traveled widely and played a vital role in the affairs of their time. They found in our shared wilderness experience something deeply satisfying that more than compensated for the hardship and work involved.

On the Churchill expedition described in this book were: Dr. Anthony J. Lovink, then Netherland's Ambassador to Canada; Major General Elliot Rodger of the Canadian Army; Eric Morse, executive director of the Associated Clubs of Canada; Dr. Omond Solandt, chairman of the Defence Research Board of Canada; and Denis Coolican, president of the Canadian Bank Note Company, Ltd.

Tony, dean of the diplomatic corps at Ottawa, had served all over the world and was steeped in the give-and-take of international affairs. He was tall, lean, and rangy. Even in his bush outfit he was a diplomat, but on the trip his greatest attributes were a philosophical turn of mind, a slight Dutch accent, and the skill with which he set up the tent he shared with me. His all-important task, however, was supplying us with what we needed in the way of fish.

Elliot had a great knowledge of the rivers and lakes of his far-flung command. Beloved of his men, compact, lithe, and adventurous, he liked white water, and to hear him laugh after running a rapids was a joy. He was possessed of boundless energy and zest. Whenever we stopped, he headed into the bush and returned with treasures—caribou horns, Indian relics, strange formations of rock or wood. But it was as second cook and helper around the fire that he really came into his own, for he had a good soldier's intuitive efficiency and sense of priorities.

Eric, student of voyageur history, was in charge of all the careful research and planning that went into the expedition. With a temperament and enthusiasm that matched Elliot's, the two made a good team, serving as scouts ranging far and wide off the trail, coming back like bird dogs to report their findings. It was Eric who roused the voyageurs each morning with the historic call *Lèvi lèvi lèvi, nos gens"* and then, no matter how cold it was, plunged into the water with much splashing. Possibly more significant, however, was his reading to us from the diaries of the explorers who had traveled our route.

Omond, with a scientist's accurate turn of mind and almost infallible judgment, was in charge of charts, logistics, and calculations. Solidly built and imperturbable, with a deep sense of humor, he had a stabilizing influence. Because of his unquestioned integrity, one of the major responsibilities was delegated to him. This was to uphold a tradition of the trade, doling out to weary voyageurs after a hard day, a meticulously calibrated dram of rum from the little "Dutchman."

Denis, formerly of the Canadian Navy, was as fluent in French as in English, his a patois and a rare sense of habitant perception no disaster could dampen. With a powerful set of shoulders that could all but lift a canoe out of the water, he was a good bowman, and to see him boring into a gale made adverse winds unimportant. When a landing was made for the night, it was his immediate task to find rocks to support the grate and kindling for the fire, and if there was any daylight left after supper, to keep the expedition's diary.

I was designated as the Bourgeois which was what the voyageurs always called their leaders in the old fur-trading days. Having once been a professional guide with wilderness experience and a background in geology and ecology, the indulgent members of our expedition insisted I be responsible for major decisions. When all was said and done, however, my real contribution was as the party's cook.

I shall not attempt to give any reactions other than my own. To try and tell how my companions felt seems to me presumptuous, but this I do know, that what I felt and saw was colored and enriched by them so that my interpretation of the country and our experiences in traveling through it is, in a sense, a composite of our combined feelings. Alone, I would have seen the country, but it would have been without the completion and joy that now is mine.

There were no heroics in our travels and we took few chances, believing that desperate adventures were the result of lack of knowledge and foolhardiness. There were few flies or mosquitoes because we deliberately chose the latter part of the summer when they were gone. Many of the portages were long and difficult, and the larger lakes were dangerous at times. We were often cold, wet, and weary, but this was the price we expected to pay and the paying itself was good. To those who have never been in the bush or traversed the wilderness hinterlands by canoe, our expedition might seem like a formidable undertaking, while to old-timers just as to the voyageurs of the past, it would be merely a routine trek.

I do not entertain the illusion that a few short expeditions into the northwest makes me an authority on the country, or that this book is an accurate, carefully documented travel guide. All I want to do is give the reader some feel of this land as we saw it and to share with him some of its rewards and the sense of fulfillment that comes to men traveling the bush together. If he can catch in addition, something of the great silences still to be found in the Lonely Land, the heightened awareness that comes with a certain amount of danger, and the sense of wilderness as a counterbalance to the tensions and pressures of our age, then I shall be happy indeed.

Omond Solandt, when asked upon his return from the Churchill why he went along, answered:

"I went along to iron out the wrinkles in my soul," which is perhaps as good an explanation as any I know for a venture such as ours.

CHAPTER I

ILE À LA CROSSE

T*HIS lake and fort take their names from . . . the game of the cross which forms a principle amusement among the natives. The situation of this lake, the abundance of the finest fish in the world to be found in its waters, the richness of its surrounding banks and forests, in moose and fallow deer* [probably Barren Ground caribou], *with the vast numbers of the smaller tribes of animals, whose skins are precious, and the numerous flocks of wild fowl that frequent it in the spring* *and fall, make it a most desirable spot for the constant residence of some and the occasional rendezvous of others of the inhabitants of the country, particularly the Kniesteneaux.*

—ALEXANDER MACKENZIE

✻

I WALKED TO the end of the dock and looked over the canoes. Their bows were snubbed to the pilings and they floated freely, pulling gently at their moorings. The packs were stowed away and I counted them once more. Extra paddles, tracking lines, map cases tied to the thwarts, fishing rods, axes, all were there. The canoes rode well, not too high in the bows, but just enough. Peterborough Prospectors were made for the bush and for roaring rapids and waves. They embodied the best features of all canoes in the north. They were wide of beam with sufficient depth to take rough water, and their lines gave them maneuverability and grace. In them was the lore of centuries, of Indian craftsmen who had dreamed and perfected the beauty of the birchbark, and of French voyageurs who also loved the feel of a paddle and the smooth glide of a canoe through the water. All this was taken by modern craftsmen who—with glues, waterproof fillers and canvas, together with the accuracy of machine-tooled ribs and thwarts, planking and gunwales—made a canoe of which Northmen might well be proud. Our three lay there in the sunshine ready to go.

Back of the dock, the marsh grass was beaten down where the packs had been thrown. I went over, walked through the patch of sedge, and kicked around with my boots to see if some small item might have fallen out. A package of salt or pepper, the first-aid kit, a compass, a reel, or a box of fishing lures, a hank of rope or twine, patching material for the canoes, the Carborundum stone for sharpening knives and axes—the loss of any one of these would cause trouble from the start. I walked back and forth, explored beneath a willow bush, and satisfied at last, returned to the canoes.

A number of Indians watched our final preparations. Corp. Albin Nelson of the Royal Canadian Mounted Police was there with his wife and Mr. and Mrs. Leonard Budgel of the Hudson's Bay Company. They had all been very kind, were used to expeditions starting off, understood how little time we had, and our need of getting swiftly underway.

Now everything was ready. Behind us was the luncheon at Prince Albert, the greetings and warnings, the photographs and interviews, the inevitable delays in getting all the gear and equipment together in one place, final messages and good-bys, the thousand-and-one necessary things that are time-consuming.

"The water is high," said Corporal Nelson, "possibly three feet above normal. You'll have to watch the rapids with the river over its banks."

"Camp on the sandspit," said Mr. Budgel. "It will be dry there."

We shook hands all around and got into the canoes—Tony and Omond in the first, Elliot and Eric in the second, Denis and I in the third. We would start that way and see how things worked out. The final decisions as to who would stay with whom was a matter of weight, strength, and endurance, something that could be determined only after several days of paddling. While the bow lines were being freed, I stood up in the stern for a final look around.

"Watch Drum Rapids," said one of the Indians. "Stay on the left after the fast water."

"Wolverine knows river," said another. "He live Patuanak."

I nodded, sat down and pushed hard against the dock. When safely out, we turned, waved good-by once more. Then paddles dug deep and we were on our way. We heard Corporal Nelson's motor and in a moment his boat swept past us and around for final pictures. We rolled in the swells, waved gaily again and then headed down the lake. We were alone on its placid surface. The Hudson's Bay Post with its scattered clusters of cabins and tents was to one side. On the dock was a black knot of figures. It was breaking up now. The Indians were going back to the village. Just back of the dock was the green airstrip carved out of the bush where we had landed only a few hours ago.

We headed for a long point a mile away, a promontory that would separate us from contact with the outside. That point was the door to the wilderness. When we rounded it, we would enter the world of Alexander Mackenzie, Peter Pond, and David Thompson, where nothing had really changed.

It felt good to be cruising again, good to feel the canoes responding to each stroke, to hear the ripple from the bow and the steady swish of our paddles. Our shirts came off and the sun beat on our backs.

Denis laughed out loud. "Bourgeois," he said, "we paddle well together, *n'est-ce pas?*"

His great shoulders bent to the work, and our canoe leaped forward. How easy to swing through a stroke without any encumbrance! Muscles were free again and so were our lungs. The air was clean with just enough coolness, and in it the smell of hundreds of square miles of spruce and waterways, muskeg and tundra, caribou moss and wet granite. Then suddenly the point was to our left and we were slipping by it into the open, with only distance and space to the north. Off to the left was Aubichon Arm reaching for Peter Pond Lake and Methye Portage on the great divide between the Churchill and the Mackenzie. Down that blue misty sweep had come the brigades of the past on their way to Grand Portage to meet the men from Montreal.

Somewhere ten miles away was our camp site, but the distance meant nothing to us then. Ten, twenty, or forty miles at the moment, it was all the same, so good did it feel to be underway again. As the vistas took hold, all else was forgotten. The warmth of the sun caressed us, and muscles that hadn't been used for a long time stretched themselves and tensed against the pull of our blades. We were seeing Ile à la Crosse as we wanted to, counting the miles and headlands as only canoemen do with time enough to absorb and study every detail of the shores. None of us said a word during those first hours. Now with open horizons to the north all we wanted was to push ahead, soak up the first impressions of a great new waterway and feel those Peterboroughs move smoothly through the water.

Eric and Elliot were far to the right, Omond and Tony to the left, their paddles moving as rhythmically as ours. Their shirts were off too. The color of those backs would change from pink and white to brown. They were unscarred now— no scratches, no welts from black flies or the "bulldogs"—but all of that would come. The canoes rode high and their reflections shimmered in the light. They seemed very small on the vast surface of the lake and at times almost disappeared in the haze that hung above it. So small and fragile did they appear that it seemed almost presumptuous to expect them to reach their destination.

Once long ago I had written:

"The movement of a canoe is like a reed in the wind. Silence is part of it, and the sounds of lapping water, bird songs, and wind in the trees. It is part of the medium through which it floats, the sky, the water, and the shores. A man is part of his canoe and therefore part of all it knows. The instant he dips his paddle, he flows as it flows, the canoe yielding to his slightest touch and responsive to his every whim and thought. . . . There is magic in the feel of a paddle and the movement of a canoe, a magic compounded of distance, adventure, solitude and peace. The way of a canoe is the way of the wilderness and of a freedom almost forgotten, the open door to waterways of ages past and a way of life with profound and abiding satisfactions."

We were in the groove again, and suddenly it seemed as though we had never been away from it. Strange how swiftly one moves into a wilderness way of life, how airplane terminals, crowds, cities, and jobs move into the background and seem unimportant compared to the fact that one is underway and on one's own. We had a camp site to find, tents to set up, gear to sort; the outfit must be whipped into shape before dark. Mr. Budgel had mentioned a sandspit somewhere down the lake, a beach off a point, and after an hour we saw it jutting out like a long brown finger from the west. We would find no rocks in the Ile à la Crosse country, no smooth shelves for landing and tent sites until we reached the Canadian Shield some days later. But a beach of any kind was better than a camp in the willows. With flood conditions on the Churchill, dry places would be scarce.

As we neared the sandspit, we had our first real glimpse of the lake's full sweep. "This is it," I kept saying to myself, "this is the Churchill country, Great Slave, Mackenzie," names that had haunted my dreams for years. "This," I said to myself, "is where you might have come half a lifetime ago had you not found the Quetico-Superior country north of Lake Superior."

The sandspit rose like a wall on the south side but leveled off toward the end of the point and on the north. Tent poles and drying racks for fish indicated an old Indian camp. The end of the spit was alive with pelicans, gulls, sandpipers, terns, and shorebirds of all kinds. Suddenly it seemed to rise, and the air was full of wings and the screaming of birds. It was our first encounter with the white pelicans; we watched them with delight as they soared in perfect wingtip formation down the lake. The smaller birds came back, reluctant to leave their feeding ground, and ran up and down close to the water's edge even when the canoes drew near. We circled the end of the point and found that on the far side where the waves came down the long sweep of the lake, the sand had been washed up level and smooth. We landed there and unloaded the canoes.

Back of the beach itself was a spot grown thickly enough with bearberry so that the sand would not get into our food and sleeping bags. I was glad to see it. A sandy camp at the beginning of an expedition can be a source of annoyance during the entire trip. No matter how careful one may be, sand always gets into everything. There was plenty of space, protection from the wind and a grand view down the lake. We would see both the sunset and the sunrise and out in the open, the birds, who were still protesting our presence.

Raspberry bushes grew in profusion. We quickly picked enough berries for supper, which would be an ample meal of fried ham, mashed potatoes, tea, and a loaf of fresh bread Mrs. Budgel had given us. There was plenty of driftwood for a fire and even before the tents were unpacked, a blaze was crackling under the old blackened pots. I sliced the ham and placed it in the frying pan, then laid out some tinned butter and jam. In half an hour supper would be ready.

The voyageurs were blowing up their air beds and laying out

their sleeping bags. Once voyageurs slept on the ground under their canoes with only a single blanket to cover them. They had no mosquito bars, no real protection should it storm. Only the Bourgeois had a tent lined with spruce boughs, but still they slept soundly—as who would not after sixteen hours of paddling and portaging. Even the ground was soft to them and when they arose what speed was theirs!

Thomas L. McKenney, according to Paul Provencher, recalled an instance from his expedition in 1826, "when his men took the canoe out of the water, mended a breach in it, reloaded, cooked breakfast, shaved, washed, ate and re-embarked, all in fifty-seven minutes." We were not that fast because we had more equipment to pack. Usually it took a couple of hours to get underway in the morning, though camp was pitched in half the time at night.

The three-man seven-by-nine Baker tent went up for Elliot, Omond, and Denis. Shaped like a wedge with the entire front open and a broad protecting fly, it was our refuge when it rained during meal times. The low rear needed no supports and the front only one sturdy pole between two sets of crosses.

Tony and I had a seven-by-seven foot "A" tent which could be strung between two trees or, if none were available, supported by the conventional set of cross poles at each end.

Eric, who likes to sleep alone, had a small explorer's pup tent. Usually his pitch required no poles at all, merely a convenient branch to hold up the front end, and bushes or pegs for the side and rear ties.

All the tents were made of closely woven, waterproofed cotton cloth. They were fitted with good mosquito bars closed with zippers. Sod cloths all around the bottom were adequate enough so they could be firmly weighted down with stones, if necessary. We did not like sewed-in bottoms, so each ground sheet was separate and could be used as a tarpaulin in case of emergency. When the air beds and sleeping bags were laid down and the ground sheet carefully tucked over the sod cloth, no flies or mosquitoes could enter.

How swiftly a place becomes home when the tents are up and a fire burning. Our shelters looked cozy and almost permanent there above the beach, and the smoke from our fire made it seem as though we had been there a long time. It was almost as though we were still on the canoe trip of the year before when we covered the La Vérendrye route and camped on the beach at Grand Portage. Blair Fraser and John Endemann had been along then. Blair was now in the Near East for *Maclean's Magazine*, John at the South African Embassy in Rome. It was hard to believe a year had passed.

After supper we sorted the outfit, getting order out of confusion by checking items of personal gear, flashlights, knives, pencils, maps, and aerial photographs. Food was all important, so we sorted out mounds of muslin bags, breakfast, lunch, supper supplies, staples, and items for immediate consumption. The extra bags of flour, rice, peas, beans, sugar, reserves of bacon, salt pork, dried fruit went into a pack we would not have to touch for a week or more. Into the lunch pack went the various items we would need each noon, the condiments, the odds and ends of equipment in constant use. It would take several days for the outfit to shake down to the point where we knew the exact location of everything. The important thing now was to place the reserves in the bottoms of the packs, the items which might be used immediately on top where they could be found without trouble or lengthy searching. In time those food bags would become so familiar in appearance and feel that I could go through them in the dark and know by a touch exactly what was in each.

I looked over the foodstuffs. What a variety compared to that of the old-time voyageurs! All they had were dried peas or corn, possibly some fat or pemmican with whatever extra they could find. Day after day and week after week it was simply that. The cook had only one pot to worry about, though it was a big one. The flour soup went in the pot, and after it was nearly cooked, whatever meat or grease was available was added. A quart of peas or corn or flour per man was the usual daily ration.

According to the 1857 journal of Peter Jacobs, a native missionary, this was their standard food.

"The food that is generally prepared and eaten in these regions by voyageurs is what is called 'ahrubuhboo.' I do not know what the word itself means. I spell it as I hear it pronounced. All pork eaters from Canada do not know how to make it; I shall here tell my readers how I proceeded to make it; for it was this sort of food we had in the voyage. After I had got the wood in order, and made a good blazing fire, I took my kettle, went to the lake, and put in it about two quarts of water. While this was getting to boil over the fire, I took a two-quart hand dish half full of water, and put into it some flour, and stirred it till it looked like mush. The pan was now full. As the water in the kettle was now boiling, I took my pan-dish, and put all that was in it in the kettle, where it became thinner. I then took a stick and stirred. This, of course took some time to boil. When it boiled, I kept stirring it in order to prevent dregs of the flour soup from sinking and sticking at the bottom of the kettle and burning.

"If it burned, the dinner would be spoiled. . . . When the flour soup was quite cooked, I removed the kettle from the fire; and while my soup was boiling hot, I jumped at my hatchet or tomahawk, and cut to pieces about a pound weight of pemmi-can, after which I threw this into the kettle. I stirred this quickly so that the grease of the pemmican might be dis-solved in the hot flour soup. Thus ends the cooking. The time it takes to cook this is less than half an hour. It is very much like what is called in some countries burgoo. This 'ahrubuhboo' is first rate food for travellers in this country. At this time I poured it out in dishes for my men and myself, and made a good dinner out of it. Very often the men, when they are in a great hurry, instead of using dishes and spoons, pour out their 'ah-rubuhboo' on the smooth and hollow rocks, where it be-comes cooler in a short time, and eat it; those who have no spoons generally eat it in dog fashion, licking it up with their tongues."

What luxury was ours compared to theirs. For breakfasts we always had bacon or fish, Red River porridge, or oatmeal cooked with raisins and served with brown sugar, dehydrated milk and always a pot of strong, black coffee. For lunches there was bread or bannock, with marmalade, cheese, corned beef or sausage and either a cold drink made of fruit crystals or tea; for supper, fish or dried meat with dehydrated vegetables and a pail of dried fruit. Any Bourgeois of two hundred years ago would have thought our supplies were a sign of softness and degeneracy. Actually the weight or the amount of bulk of our food, most of it dehydrated, was not much more than theirs, nor did it take any longer to prepare. We carried only enough food for two weeks. We could replenish our supplies at Stanley Post halfway down the Churchill. Approximately two pounds per man per day compared favorably with the weight of the standard ration of a quart of dried peas with some pork or fat for each voyageur in the days of the brigades.

After supper Tony and I went for a paddle. The water was already tinted by the sunset. It was too weedy and shallow for fishing, so we sat in the canoe a mile away from camp and listened. We had a tradition of after-supper paddles, he and I, and no matter if we had traveled all day and were dog-tired, if possible we pushed off for a final half hour before rolling in. In a sense it was a luxury not to have any particular objective, and those last moments of idle drifting seemed a good way to end the day. We sat there in the glow and looked back toward the sandspit. The tents were very tiny and the smoke from our fire rose straight into the sky. There was no movement around camp, no lifting of wings, no sound of screaming birds.

"Bourgeois," said Tony, "it is good to be here, very good," and I knew what it meant for him to be away from the world of diplomatic functions, the endless whirl of social life in the capital, the delicate balancing of personalities and values, his ever-present responsibilities.

That night it seemed good to crawl into our sleeping bags, to lie there again and listen. Once I heard the howl of a husky dog from an Indian camp down the shore. At first I thought it might be a wolf, forgetting at the moment we were within ten miles of the post. I had seen tracks in the sand and had wondered. But the howl settled it. This was the land of the Crees and huskies and their music would be a part of every Indian camp we would pass. As we drifted off to sleep I could hear the wind rising behind us to the south, just a soft whispering over the sand, but enough to tell me that things were stirring. If it continued, by dawn we might have a gale behind us for the thirty-mile run to the end of the lake.

CHAPTER 2

ATHABASCA BRIGADE

Norway House, 16the August 1820

TO WM. WILLIAMS ESQRE.,
Governor in Chief of Ruperts Land

SIR:

I HAVE *the Honor to acquaint you that the Athabasca and Peace River Brigades took their departure from hence yesterday morning; much time has been lost from the want of proper subordination amongst the people, and it is with the utmost difficulty we have been enabled to bring them to their duty, they now however promise well and the Guides assure me they will make up for the delay that has taken place. . . . Our Compliment is twelve canoes navigated by sixty men, contg. two hundred and fifty four pieces, which I suspect is far short of what the Department requires, we must make the most of everything, and as Isle à la*

35

THE LONELY LAND

Crosse is overstocked with goods, I expect Mr. Clarke will furnish us with a supply of such articles as we stand most in need of during the winter.

—GEORGE SIMPSON

❧

I WAS UP before the east began to glow and in the half light of dawn stood down at the beach watching the whitecaps racing past the point and rolling on toward the north. There was a tail wind, and the day would be good. We should be at the head of the lake by late afternoon. What luck, for if the wind had been against us we would have to fight our way down that long unbroken stretch toward Patuanak and the Drum. We could easily have been wind-bound and forced to spend precious hours waiting for a break.

I gathered long shreds of birchbark from a broken tree and driftwood tossed up by the waves of some previous storm. It was tinder-dry, for it had been in the sun and the winds had blown over it as it lay high on the sands. Soon a bright fire was crackling under the grill. The pots went on and breakfast was underway, not exactly a voyageur's repast, for we were still close enough to civilization to enjoy fresh eggs and back bacon, canned fruit, and what was left of the loaf of fresh bread. While I made everything ready, the tents came down and all the packing was done except the food and cooking outfit.

As we ate, some of the birds came back screaming in protest

36

and landed, only to take off again. The pelicans soared over us, then disappeared down the lake. The terns and gulls circled and dipped. Only the shorebirds ran up and down the sand following the ebb and flow of the waves as though we we were not there.

"The pelicans don't like us," said Denis. "Did you see their expressions? For all the world like looking at us over the tops of their spectacles."

I laughed. "They seem to take a dim view of our entire operation. The canoes are too new, our backs the wrong color, and we've disrupted their feeding."

"Give us time," he said. "A few more days and we'll fit into the scenery like the Crees themselves."

We cleaned up the cooking outfit, packed it away, put out the fire, stowed the packs in the canoes and made a final check of the tent sites. Everything was in order. We stood at the water's edge ready to take off.

"Thirty miles to go," announced Omond, after consulting his map. "With this gale we should make the end of the lake by nightfall."

Ile à la Crosse was important in the old days. Everyone came through who traveled into the Northwest. Down this broad stretch the canoes had headed for Athabasca and the Mackenzie; to Ile à la Crosse had come the brigades from Saskatchewan to the south. Here was a crossroads of travel as well-known in the West as Grand Portage on Lake Superior.

Mackenzie made these notations coming through upstream:

"Then Shagoina strait and rapid lead into the Lake of Ile à la Crosse, in which the course is south twenty miles, and south-south-west fourteen miles, to the Point au Sable; opposite to which is the discharge of the Beaver-River, bearing south six miles; the lake in the distance run does not exceed twelve miles in its greatest breadth. It now turns west-south-west, the Isle à la Crosse being on the south, and the mainland on the north; and it clears the one and the other in the distance of three miles, the water presenting an open horizon to right and left; that on the left formed by a deep narrow bay, about ten leagues in depth; and that to the right by what is called la Riviere Creuse, or Deep River, being a canal of still water which is here four miles wide. On following the last course, Isle à la Crosse Fort appears on a low isthmus, at the distance of five miles, and it is in latitude 55.25. North, and longitude 107. West."

Our canoes were birchbarks that morning, freshly gummed for the rapids and waves ahead, my partners voyageurs, bronzed, bearded, and burned from wintering in the Athabasca country. They were on their way to Grand Portage to meet old friends, to eat fresh bread again, to dance to the fiddles in the Great Hall, to fight heroic battles on the beach and to do the things they could boast about for a year to come.

We had plenty of freeboard and as we began to ride the swells from the south, feeling the lift and power of them, the men of the old brigades rode with us. That morning there were songs in the wind: *En roulant ma boule, La Belle Lizette, La Claire Fontaine*. In the sound of the rising wind we could hear them.

En roulant ma boule roulant,
En roulant ma boule
En roulant ma boule roulant
En roulant ma boule.

The steady rhythm became part of my own stroke and unconsciously I followed the pace they set. Suddenly Denis began to sing the favorite chanson of all voyageurs:

"A la claire fontaine
M'en allant promener,
J'ai trouvé l'eau si belle
Que je m'y suis bangné.
Lui ya longtemps que je t'aime,
Jamais je ne t'oublierai."

The others joined in and as we paddled down the lake, more than ever we became a part of the ancient scene. The vistas were the same, the promontories, the new moon paling behind us, the sparkling waves, the wild crying of gulls and terns. This was the Northwest, this part of the long trail we had begun the summer before.

Our three canoes were almost abreast now, no more than a stone's throw apart. Each time a long roller came they lifted, poised for a moment, slipped down into the trough, only to rise again. Peterborough Prospectors were made for days like this. With the gale behind them, they were making better than four miles an hour, possibly five or even six if the wind held. Suddenly our canoe lifted higher than before and we hung poised

39

on a white hissing comber. As we slipped downward into the
trough, spray covered the canoe and Denis flinched as the
cold water struck his bare back.

"Bourgeois," he yelled, "I used to feel that on the bridge but
then I had my oilskins on."

I looked around for the other canoes. No longer abreast, at
times they all but disappeared and were hidden by spray. From
the vantage point of a canoe riding with a gale, the lives we
had known seemed strangely remote. Within a matter of a day
and a night, a change had come to all of us, a change no one
noticed at the time because it was so natural. This we knew
from long experience was one of the great compensations of
all wilderness expeditions. What was important was that we
were heading down the historic trail of Alexander Mackenzie
by canoe, that the wind was in our favor and that there was a
chance for a camp that night at the far end of the lake. The future to us was Drum Rapids, Deer, and Leaf and many fast waters that had no names.

A little rocky island ahead seemed to be covered with white
and had it been late fall we would have guessed it was a mantle
of snow. As we neared however, we saw it was completely
hidden by the closely packed bodies of pelicans, so close together that nowhere did the rocks show through. Suddenly the
far edge of the mantle began to lift and peeled off slowly to the
other end. For a moment sunlight glittered on a milling confusion of snowy wings, and then the great birds took off in
sedate formation toward the far shore.

Two of them left the main flock and soared toward us

wing tip to wing tip as perfectly co-ordinated in their movements as veteran pilots maneuvering together. They flew directly over us once and then again and seemingly satisfied with their reconnaissance, soared back to the flock which was resting some distance ahead.

Four hours later and possibly twenty miles from our starting point there was a slight shift in the wind, a barely perceptible shift at first, an indefinite quartering as though it could not quite make up its mind what to do. At first I thought it might be due to its veering around an island or a point, but gradually its direction changed until it was almost broadside. We watched with apprehension, hoping it was only a temporary diversion or a swirl which would finally settle down into the steady wind we had coasted with that far. More and more it swung. Rounding a sharp promontory, we found that long, uneasy swells were moving against us. Before we had gone a mile, those swells became waves with whitecaps and we knew our work was cut out for us. Still more than ten miles to go and if we were to maintain our schedule, we would have to fight every foot of the way.

We stopped for our noon snack in the lee of a small boulder-strewn island, feasted on hardtack, summer sausage, and cheese, and washed it down with a drink of lemonade. This was topped with a handful of raisins and a square of hard chocolate. As we sat munching our rations, the waves grew steadily higher. Omond checked his chart carefully.

"About ten miles of fighting the wind," he said. "We'll hug the east shore and take advantage of what cover there is."

"Let's go," I said, as soon as the lunch pack was stowed in my canoe. "In another hour this island will be awash." Already some of the biggest waves were covering us with spray.

All afternoon we fought the waves, dodged behind points and islands and any features of the shoreline that gave us protection. What a beating birchbark canoes would have taken on such a day! Seams would have needed calking to stop the trickles coming through, and packs might have become wet. With canvas canoes we had no worry, and the Peterboroughs rode the biggest waves without shipping a drop. Instead of making four or five miles an hour, however, we were now slowed to a pace of two or less.

We could have hired an Indian with a motor-driven canoe and covered the ground in half the time, and for a moment as I watched the canoes battling their way down the storm-tossed lake I wondered if we had been wise. But I knew if we had taken a tow we would have lost what we had come to find— the feeling of a great waterway and the men who traversed it long before our time. Theirs was a slow pace with time to absorb the terrain itself, its smells and sights and sounds, the intangible impressions that come only when a man moves slowly under his own power across the face of the earth. Like them, we were a brigade moving toward Cumberland House.

At last we saw the dim outlines of the low shore at the end of the lake, a swampy expanse where it turned toward Lake Shagwenaw and our second camp. For three hours more we paddled desperately and then hove to in the protection of a final point. There we turned and looked for the last time down the forty-mile stretch of Ile à la Crosse. We were weary, ready to make camp anywhere, but still had several miles to go. Hugging the shore we turned east into the swift channel of a narrows, ran our first rapids.

The smooth current emptied into the lake. There before us was the little Indian settlement of Patuanak, the thin white spire of a tiny church, the clustered shacks, tents and fish-drying racks of another Cree community. The dogs howled long before we were near, a sound that was to become so much a part of the Lonely Land that never again would we hear it without thinking of the Churchill. While we had known we would find the village and its mission, somehow it seemed incongruous to have them materialize. This was particularly true of the church, even though it was now as much a part of the life of this waterway as the Hudson's Bay Posts themselves. As we neared, we could see the bright red flag over the company store and the freshly painted house of the clerk set back of the compound. We pushed into the dock, were met by a crowd of curious children, several women and older people, and one who looked like a dwarf.

They looked at us in amazement. It was a strange thing for white men to be paddling canoes. Everyone used large freighters and motors. Even the poorest Indian wanted some sort of mechanized transport. The canoe might be broken and patched, the motor of ancient vintage, held together with wire and rope and bits of tin, but at least it meant he didn't have to paddle. Paddling was for fishing off the major waterways, for women and children and muskrat trappers, certainly not for major expeditions down the Churchill. It was inconceivable anyone would travel this way for pleasure.

Our pack sacks were interesting to them for since the days of the old brigades most carrying had been done by the time-honored method of a tump line and harness. The tump line itself is merely a broad leather strap from which extend several long thongs. The article to be carried is usually wrapped in a tarpaulin, tied with the thongs, the actual carrying being done with the strap across the forehead. If the first bundle fits neatly against the small of the back, other pieces can be placed on top, and the weight will rest on the back and shoulders, with the real strain on the head.

This was the way voyageurs carried their standard load of two *pièces*, or 180 pounds, and they spoke with awe of some who had carried five and even eight at one time. The tradition continues, for Paul Provencher speaks of one "Harry Pitlegans, a Montagnais half-breed who on a bet in 1927 carried over six hundred pounds of flour ankle deep in soft sand for a quarter of a mile."

All of this had always been done with the tump line and harness, and the Indians knew its history. No wonder they looked at our packs with astonishment. True they also had a head strap, but the actual carrying was done with shoulder straps. Mackenzie, when speaking of transporting goods across the nine miles of Grand Portage, paid the voyageur a high compliment when he said:

"When they arrived at Grand Portage, which is near nine miles over, each of them had to carry eight packages of such goods and provisions as are necessary for the interior country. This is a labor which cattle cannot conveniently perform in summer as both horses and oxen were tried by the company without success."

Of greatest interest was my pack basket in which I carried lunches, a lightweight woven box of red-pine strips built to fit snugly into one of the packs and stiff enough so that bannock, eggs, jam, or any breakables could be carried safely. In that basket went the tea pail, six cups, salt and pepper and the snacks we would need for the noon meal. The Indians had known the grub box but they had never seen a device like this. Both served the same purpose, did away with the necessity of searching for items of food or undoing a regular pack during the day. When the time came to eat, only that one box or pack had to be undone. It always rode in my canoe and no one else carried it.

One look at the cluttered shoreline and the ravenous dogs, and we decided not to stop. Even though the shores beyond looked low and swampy there must be some place better than the village. I wanted to go to the post, however, to exchange some of our unsmoked Canadian back bacon—which an unknowing clerk had decided we needed—for the heavily smoked bush variety. There is little fat on back bacon and we knew that within a week, being uncured, it would become tainted. So we laid in a supply of the brown boardlike slabs which would keep indefinitely, no matter what the weather.

Back again at the dock we asked the dwarf, who was very talkative, about the Indian known as Wolverine whom we

had been told knew more about the river than anyone else.
"He fly away," said the dwarf, "far, far away." And he
pointed to the east. "Two days ago he fly."

We had been told at Ile à la Crosse that a fire was raging
somewhere beyond Primeau and we knew a government plane
had come in and picked up a crew. When I asked about a camping place, he said: "Good camp on beach."

"What about a rocky place?" I asked.

He laughed. "No stones, no stones any place. Why?"

The answer to that simple question was far too difficult and
involved for me to attempt a reply. All I said was: "We like
rocks better than swamp and trees."

I knew that did not make much of an impression. It was beyond them why we did not go down to the beach and camp
back of the rushes or pitch our tents right where we were like
everyone else. Crazy white men paddling canoes, funny pack
sacks and queer notions about where to stop for the night.

The voyageurs of the old brigades would not have scorned
the village and the post, and no doubt they had stopped there
many times in the past. Husky dogs, thieving children, flies and
dirt and noise would not have disturbed them in the least. They
would have turned over their big birchbark canoes, built a fire
near the shore and made merry with the Indians, but then their
needs had been somewhat different from ours. While we
sought to escape even little native settlements and be as much
on our own as possible, to them any sort of a gathering after
their long and arduous travels was a welcome relief from lone-
liness and monotony.

CHAPTER 3

THE SHIELD

B y civilised men, especially
those of the United States, who have a mortal antipathy to the
North American Indian; or as he is called, the "Red Man"; it is
confidently predicted that the Red Man, must soon cease to
exist, and give place to the White Man; this is true of all the lands
formerly possessed by the Red Man; that the White Man has
thought it worth his while to seize by fraud or force; but the
Stony-Region is an immense extent of country, on which the

White Man cannot live; except by hunting, which he will not submit to. Here then is an immense tract of country, which the Supreme Being, the Lord of the whole earth has given to the Deer, and other wild animals; and to the Red Man forever, here, as his fathers of many centuries past have done, he may roam free as the wind; but this wandering life, and the poverty of the country prevents the labors of the Missionary to teach them the sacred truths of Christianity.

—DAVID THOMPSON (*1796*)

PATUANAK, ACCORDING TO our geological maps, was off the edge of the Shield and it was just possible that there wasn't a rocky camp site anywhere around. Surely, I reasoned, the Indians would know. Having lived in a low, swampy area where the only elevations were deposits of glacial sand and gravel, a granite ledge would be remembered. When the young clerk came down to see us off, we asked him, too, but he simply shook his head and said as far as he knew, there were no such camping places on the lake.

"Is there anyone," I asked him finally, "now that Wolverine is gone, who can tell us about the rapids coming up?"

He shook his head again. "No one left," he said, "who has been over that way."

We would have to tackle the Drum with what meager knowledge we had. Once more we looked over the area of the landing, finally decided anything would be better than camping there. A look at the beach the dwarf had mentioned was discouraging. In the bull rushes and washed up against the sand were dead suckers swarming with flies; the stench of their rotting pervaded the entire bay. Back of the beach was a dense growth of willows deep in water, and beyond them, small aspen and spruce. The whole area was a dank and putrid swamp. The wind was down now, so we pushed off hurriedly and headed for the open lake.

Before we had gone a mile, Omond and Tony called and pointed to an orange spot on a promontory to the west. Though off course, it was worth investigating. Through the glasses the spot looked like an overturned boat or possibly the abandoned pontoon of a plane, but the more I studied it and its background, the more I became convinced it might be a rocky shelf.

Suddenly Tony yelled: "Rock, solid rock!"

Improbable as it seemed it might be a lone outcropping which extended from some formation in the North. Such islands and promontories were not uncommon in the low country, and time and again I had found ledges in great expanses of bog. The closer we drew the more it looked like a shelf, low at its tip to be sure, but rising steadily back from the water's edge. A mile farther on we stopped again, looked once more with the glasses. The orange spot was taking shape not as a boat or a plane pontoon, but very definitely as a ledge covered with orange lichens flaming in the last rays of the setting sun, the whole promontory a bold invasion of the Canadian Shield.

Our three canoes began to race. Weariness was forgotten in

that final dash, the miles down Ile à la Crosse, the head winds we had fought since noon. The sight of the Shield gave us new strength and the realization we would soon be on it again and know the clean glaciated surfaces we had found in the Quetico was a lift to our spirits. The canoes fairly boiled through the water. Tony and Omond were now in the lead, Eric and Elliot next, Denis and I in the rear.

The point now seemed to be on fire, as did the entire ledge in back of it. It looked as though someone had taken a brush and streaked it with brilliant orange paint. The spot we had first seen was a table of rock supported by several boulders. Back of that were sloping shelves, one above the other, commanding a view of the west and the village. This was good fortune, far more than we had hoped for. We landed below the first shelf, unloaded the canoes and carried them well up from the water. The rocks felt good to our feet.

"Beach good place," said Denis, quoting the dwarf; "no rocks anywhere."

We built the fireplace down near the water while the others scoured the ledges for tent sites and vistas. It was quiet and clean and we were alone. Stiff, pinnacled spruce was the skyline toward the Drum in contrast to the soft outlines of aspen, birch, and willow down the lake. If our maps were correct and the Churchill followed the edge of the Shield, we might have good camp sites for the rest of the trip.

That night by way of celebration I decided to cook a special stew. When the water in the big pot had come to a rolling boil, I dropped in two generous handfuls of dehydrated potatoes and onions, opened up one of the precious tins of tomato concentrate and a package of dried beef noodle soup. When the mixture was simmering, I emptied into it three cakes of the compressed dried meat the Canadian Army was perfecting for its use as emergency rations in the field, something so close to the old pemmican in flavor and content that only an expert could tell the difference. As I stirred gently, I seasoned the stew with salt and pepper and a few bay leaves. By the time the tents were up, it was almost done and the entire area was rich with its fragrance. I shifted the bannock so it would bake and brown, then stood to one side admiring my efforts.

Omond was busy concocting a brew out of rum and lemon crystals, a practice old-timers would have scorned. We sat in a row along the lower ledge and drank a toast to the Shield. Across the lake was the village, the tiny white church, and the red roof of the Hudson's Bay Company store. Plumes of smoke from many fires blended with the rozy haze of sunset. We had been lucky enough to beat the wind in spite of its change of direction. Even though we knew that tomorrow we would encounter our first rapids, morning was a long way off. I looked over the Voyageurs with pride—Tony, Eric, Elliot, Omond, and Denis. Forty miles by the second day, and that with muscles soft and not used to swinging a paddle. We were back on a bit of the Shield. That alone would have been reason enough for satisfaction. We might have made out all right back in the willows or on some spruce-grown rise away from the lake, but it wouldn't have been the same. So long had the Shield been part of us and so fond had we become of what it meant that for the rest of our lives we thought we would never feel quite as happy as when upon it.

Even though what we had found was only an outcrop of the Shield in a great area of bog and glacial till, it was part of the whole and from this tiny fragment all the rest stood clear. Spreading over the north half of the continent, with Hudson Bay its center, its fringes embossed with names that spoke of far frontiers, Yellow Knife, Flin Flon, and Chibougamau. "Eight hundred years ago," according to Blair Fraser in *Maclean's Magazine*, "when Leif Ericson the Viking saw it first he called it Helluland, the land of flat stone. Jacques Cartier reported to King Francis I of France that there is not a cartload of dirt in the whole of it." So inhospitable was this land that for two centuries any thought of Canadian expansion to the north or across it toward the west seemed foolhardy. Yet the Shield more than any other part of Canada had been responsible for its industrial growth. From its two million square miles come copper, iron, nickel, uranium, and cobalt for the atomic age, from its swift rivers unlimited sources of power, from its forests pulp and lumber.

I left the ledge and went back to the fire. The stew needed stirring, and a little seasoning. When it was done, I set it to one side on the smooth rock. That rock was scoured by the same glacial ice that had covered the rest of the Shield, had been washed by rains and the melting freshets of spring. Its clean hardness meant more to me than its hidden wealth. So strong had this feeling become in all of us that in lowlands or swamps or even in sedimentary formations, there was always a desire to escape and find it wherever it might be. This is the charm of the Quetico-Superior and of Ontario and Quebec. On many occasions we had paddled miles for the simple privilege of feeling it under our feet and seeing its stark, haunting beauty.

Before me were several long straight grooves running almost north and south. They had been cut by rocks held in the glacier's base. Scattered over the ledges were huge boulders dropped there by the melting ice, and across the bay in back of the village were ridges of moraine. The Shield had not changed much since the last retreat of the ice some ten thousand years ago; it looks today much as it did when the hairy mammoth roamed its frozen fastnesses during the last ice age. Those glacial scratches before me were almost as fresh as when the gigantic mass of ice and debris ground across the land, gouging out lake beds, leveling and smoothing the roots of ancient mountains, changing drainage patterns, and scouring out valleys. The forty-mile gash of Ile à la Crosse, though covered with glacial debris, had no doubt been made that way, and so had most of the lakes we would cover in our route.

Under my feet was greenstone, the oldest rock in the world, formed by the erosion of the earth's original crust, compacted into sediments that in turn were changed through the vast pressures and heat of volcanic action. On either side were granites, gneisses, and veins of snowy quartz. They had boiled up as lavas and gases from the interior through fissures in the mother rock.

The entire ledge was overgrown with mosses and lichens, bearberry and juniper, and down in a little cleft was a clump of gnarled and withered birch. We could as well have been on a rock in the Quetico-Superior, or a thousand miles farther north. During the years we had known the Shield we had absorbed a certain sense of oneness with its spruce and jack pine, its granite and caribou moss, muskeg and Labrador tea, Linnaea and dwarf dogwood. Everywhere the vegetation was somewhat the same and what was true of plants was also true of birds and other forms of life. This was the land of moose and caribou, of the wolf and the wolverine, the Canadian jay and the spruce hen. No matter what lay ahead the Shield could not be entirely strange. With its sense of timelessness, its old familiar beauty, it would always be our type of country and we would always feel at home there.

Anyone who has seen Alexander Jackson's painting "First Snow, Georgian Bay" or James MacDonald's "The Solemn Land" knows it is different from any other part of the continent. The Canadian artists known as "The Group of Seven" caught its fierce simplicity on canvas; they devoted their lives to capturing its boldness, space and far horizons.

Blair Fraser said: "Man has made little impression on this land and civilization almost none. Until aerial photography came into its own after World War II less than half of it had ever been mapped. To this day it is not thoroughly explored. Almost anywhere on its rough face, it is easy to imagine yourself alone in both space and time."

I thought of all these things as I put the finishing touches to our evening meal. The tea was ready and I took it off the fire to steep. I set the fruit in the water to cool. The bannock was brown and crisp. Now I could call the others from their meditations.

"Come and get it!" I yelled and the voyageurs helped themselves to generous plates of stew, went back to the ledge, sat in a row, and wolfed it down.

The sunset over the little Indian settlement was startling. One of the last level rays caught the tip of the church spire and made it burst into flame for an instant. A faint chorus of dogs drifted to us across the water. It was a beautiful scene, but we were far too sleepy and tired to enjoy it for long.

It was dusk by the time we had stowed away the packs, checked the canoes and the outfit, covered everything against a possible rain, and weighted down ponchos and tarps with rocks. Should the wind come up, we would be at its mercy. Tent ropes must be tight, everything secured against a blow.

We crawled into our tents and into our sleeping bags, lay there for a delicious moment before closing our eyes. Far off I thought I heard a dull roar. Perhaps it was the wind, or the Drum or Dipper or any one of the many rapids that were waiting for us in the morning.

CHAPTER 4

WHITE HORSES

IT *is difficult to find in life any event which so effectually condenses intense nervous sensation into the shortest possible space of time as does the work of shooting, or running an immense rapid. There is no toil, no heart breaking labour about it, but as much coolness, dexterity, and skill as man can throw into the work of hand, eye, and head; knowledge of when to strike and how to do it; knowledge of water and rock, and of the one hundred combinations which rock and water can assume—for these two things, rock and water, taken in the abstract, fail as completely to convey any idea of their fierce embracings in the throes of a rapid as the fire burning quietly in a drawing-room fireplace fails to convey the idea of a house wrapped and sheeted in flames.*

—Sir William Francis Butler (*1872*)

I AWAKENED once during the night and lay thinking of the approaching day and the warnings we had had. Running rapids in familiar country is one thing, running them in a strange land where rock formations as well as the speed and depth of the water are different, is another.

While we were skirting the Shield and felt at home upon it, even so in the course of a thousand miles there is much to be learned. The Churchill was in flood. We had seen that at the dock, and when a river is high and out of bounds old landmarks mean nothing and there is always the danger of sweepers—windfalls with their scraggly tops reaching out like great brooms from newly eroded banks and catching anything that comes by. One bad move in white water and the expedition could end before it really got underway. We had asked about the rapids at Ile à la Crosse, had maps and notes from the Hudson's Bay Company as well as enlarged aerial photographs—all the data we could muster—but still we were not sure what to expect or what we would have to do.

The Indians traveling with their big canoes did not seem to understand what rivers could do to such little craft as ours and many of them for a generation or more had not been far from the posts. I remembered what one of them had said when questioned about a bad stretch of river.

"Oh, yes, I remember," he said, "my grandfather went there many years ago. 'Bad river,' he told us, 'very bad river.'"

All this went through my mind as I lay there listening to the dull roar to the north. I knew the sound was worse at night and that the anticipation of any rapids that have never been seen can make an old canoeman blanch if it is loud enough. The Drum was still miles away. Perhaps what I heard was the wind coming up and not the water at all. Still the roar persisted and then I knew it was not the wind for there was no moaning in the jack pines back of the tent.

The morning dawned clear and calm and the east was red with the sunrise. But the sound was still there, rising and falling, sometimes almost inaudible. Everyone was conscious of it, although during breakfast there was no mention of the Drum, the Leaf, or the Dipper.

George Simpson coming upstream in 1820 had merely mentioned them.

"Embarked before day break, ascended a bad Rapid and broke our canoe at six A.M.; which detained us about an hour. Made decharge de grand Chaguina, Portage Sonnant. Blowing hard with heavy rain. Mounted Shaguina Rapids, passed through the lake of that name, sailed through Ile à la Crosse with a fair wind and got to Fort Superior at twelve o'clock P.M."

Through my mind ran bits of advice we had had at the post: "Run the first part of Drum which is only fast water, but portage the rapids below. Remember the river is high and landings hidden. Watch out for windfalls and logs."

We studied the maps once more, loaded the canoes, tied the packs to the thwarts as we always did before running a rapids, and headed for the outlet three miles away. The white spear of the little mission looked no bigger than a spruce top and the shelters around it soon faded into the background of the low shore. The faint howl of a husky drifted to us as we slipped into the channel on our way to the river. Within half an hour the bay narrowed and now there was a perceptible movement of the water. The sound we had heard gradually became an all-engulfing roar. It submerged the rising wind, the swish of paddles and the chuckles from the bow. As we moved into its center the old tight feeling within me grew, a feeling I have never overcome and possibly never will. Others may say they approach fast water with calm and assurance, but with me it is always the same. There was no escaping now, no turning back.

"White Horses!" yelled Tony, and down below we could see the first of the silver spouts rising and falling. He had named them well back in the Quetico days. Now they were prancing before us again. The flow became swifter and swifter. Long streamers of waterplants pointed straight ahead. There was no question of where to go; the current took care of that. The bank was in flood and the river raced through submerged clumps of willows and debris. This was dangerous for we could not tell what lay underneath, with the old scoured-out channel nowhere to be seen.

The canoe raced ahead toward a melee of rocks with stumps and windfalls lodged against them. Denis reached far to the right, pulled the bow to one side, then to the left, and again to the right. Only he could see what lay ahead and as bowman his decisions were swift and final. The instant I saw him reach or swing the bow with a swift jerk of the paddle against the front gunwale, I followed with supporting action from the stern. We dodged from one tangle to another, each time slipping by smoothly without grazing obstructions.

So far all had gone well and as we sped on our confidence grew. This was the easy part according to the Indians, the place of fast water before the real rapids of the Drum began. As the speed increased, I began to wonder what it would be like below, how we could possibly find the portage in such a raging flood and if we did find it in time, how we could check our plunge in time to portage.

There was no choice now, no thinking back to what we might have done. We were committed. I glanced hurriedly over my right shoulder. Elliot and Eric in their customary bravado were shooting straight down the river. Expert canoemen with much white-water experience, their very nonchalance frightened me. Eric looked very stern and competent; Elliot was laughing out loud.

Omond and Tony were slightly to their left, also heading down the center. That was wise, perhaps, as there the water would be deepest. Omond was an old hand and a veteran of many rivers. Tony knew more about polo ponies than canoes, but he had the balance, poise, and sensitivity of a ballet master; a good team, they would come through.

Our own canoe was hurtling down much closer to the bank and Denis, who now placed his faith in the Good Saint of all Voyageurs, handled his paddle as though it were a spear, thrusting and feinting, pushing and pulling and at times even backing water to give me a chance to pull the craft around when the speed of the current made it seem as though we could not change our course. When he indicated a move, I backed him instantly with a thrust or twist of my own.

Now there were more rocks and swirls ahead, masses of floating willow brush with islands of muskeg torn from the bogs, all moving downstream in grand confusion. A final cluster of spouts, a last desperate surge to one side, and then we were milling around together in a big eddy down below, all breathless and excited with our first taste of the Churchill.

"Bourgeois," said Denis, "we still have three canoes and we are all alive. We need put no crosses on the bank."

The real rapids of the Drum were below, with the portage supposedly on the left. At least that was the way it looked from where we sat. The legend on the Hudson's Bay Company map had said: "Natives shoot, others portage." That meant no shooting without knowing the rocks and ledges hidden beneath the flood.

We found the beginning of the portage shortly afterward, threw on the packs and canoes and sloshed along through a swamp, over rocks, and around new windfalls carried down by the river. It seemed good to be there on the ground no matter what the condition of the trail, for now the roar was deafening and the white horses spouting high and wild. At its end we loaded the canoes again and coasted a churning millrace for half a mile before we left the Drum.

Leaf Rapids was now ahead and here the legend said: "Portage just above and to the left, but can be shot by good canoemen and with care." Care was underlined. That meant us, with our prowess with canoes and our ability to read water in flood and messed up with floating vegetation. I was in the lead, the other canoes now holding back to see what I would do. As I drew close, the spouts below looked desperate. So thick were they it was impossible to see any sort of channel in between them. We skirted the drop and shot toward the left bank and when close to the shore turned into a narrow V, because of the growing swiftness of the current.

No sooner had we started down than the canoe leaped into the air and there was a sharp, sickening crack. To an old canoe-man this is the most frightening sound in the world, for it means that you have hit a rock head on. But there was no time for reflection or even fear. In an instant we were off the ledge, dodging rocks and debris. No water was spurting in, which meant the canvas was still sound.

The other men, having seen what happened to us, took a channel still farther out and our three canoes moved down the river, zigzagging between boulders and spouting rocks. Swifter and swifter went the canoes, picking V's of smooth water and avoiding white horses and waves. There was good going ahead. Now we were a team, the stern paddle sensing what the bow would do, responding to every movement no matter how slight. Near the end was a rough-looking barricade with no apparent opening. We approached cautiously, and just as we had decided not to take a chance but head for the bank, Denis noticed a rift just big enough to take us, with a smooth slick running beyond. Instantly we turned and with a swoosh shot through the opening, and then we were at the bottom with the others milling around in the foam-laced whirl-pools and looking back in half-frightened amazement at the wild staircase down which we had come.

Each canoe had suffered slight damage, but we were proud that we had come through as well as we did.

"That was fun," said Elliot, as he mopped up the water in the bottom of his canoe.

Omond had hauled out his map and was studying it care-fully. I paddled over and Denis took hold of his gunwale.

"Deer Rapids coming up," he said, " 'No portage here,' says the legend, 'but can be shot by good canoe men or voya-geurs.' "

"Well," said Eric, "what do you think, Bourgeois?"

I shrugged my shoulders. "Let's wait and see."

By now we were skeptical of all advice. If no portage was marked, the rapids were usually run. We would look it over, pick a route as we had done before and shoot. This was not an easy thing to do with the river high, we had discovered, for channels ran off through the trees and over obstructions that were not marked on the maps or in the experience of those who had gone down during periods of normal flow. It became increasingly difficult to tell where the real river bank began. Whatever we did would have to depend on how the water looked when we approached the drop.

Outcroppings of the Shield had disappeared again and the shores were swampy and low. This was why the river seemed to be running all over the woods. Deer Rapids was evidently far away, for we could hear nothing and could see no spouts in the distance. We soon forgot its threat in watching the growing number of terns and gulls wheeling and screaming above us. For a while, we forgot that Deer would have to be run before we could make our camp that night.

We stopped for lunch at an old Indian camp ground, where not long ago a moose had been killed and eaten. Bones and offal lay all around, and the flies were having a field day. After lunch we unloaded the canoes and examined them carefully. No great damage had been suffered, though there were broken ribs and planking. There was not a tear anywhere in the canvas, thanks to rounded glacial boulders instead of sharp broken ledges. All of this had happened at the head of Leaf Rapids.

After a rapids such as we had run, a voyageur's brigade would no doubt have had to make repairs on their birchbark canoes. Upon reaching shore they would have built a fire immediately and put the blackened pitch pot on to boil. If gum was running low they would have gathered more from the spruces. If there was a big tear in the bark, they might need fine spruce roots for sewing and if the rolls of bark they carried were short, they would strip some from a birch tree, fashioning it with their knives, sewing it swiftly into place, then smearing or gumming it with the melted resin until it was water-tight.

So expected was this process of gumming and repair, so valuable the necessary materials, that diaries often stated: "The canoes are in very bad condition, the cargo getting wet. Unless we stop and gum before going on, trade goods may be ruined."

Rapids broke the seams of brittle, hardened gum. Rocks bruised or tore the bark. Even large waves would cause the seams to give way. But so expert were the voyageurs in making repairs that little time was lost. With us a tube of ambroid or rubber cement and a bit of muslin or spare canvas would take care of any tears. All that was necessary was to dry the surface around the tear, scrape it clean with a knife or bit of sandpaper, and cover the entire area to be repaired with a thin layer of ambroid or cement. When at its stickiest, due to exposure to the air, a patch cut to size would be pressed smoothly down upon it and then covered with a generous layer of cement to protect the surface. This operation took only a few moments. So far we had been lucky.

As we assessed the damage we thought about the map with its legend of the Deer. "Can be shot by good canoemen," it said. We had considered ourselves reasonably expert, but when I looked at the fractured ribs in my canoe, I began to wonder. A broken canoe would be a tragedy. We simply had to come through without further injury. We would line the canoes down if we had to, swim with them if there were no footing or the water too deep and fast to wade, but down we must go through Deer and many more before we reached Flin Flon, or possibly Cumberland House.

The river now was fairly alive with birds. It seemed at times as though there were thousands in the air, wheeling and dipping, and screaming constantly. I had the feeling that they too were part of the flood, that they and the land, the water, and the air were all moving along together. So strong did this sense of fluidity become that the canoes themselves seemed part of the river with the soaring and flashing of wings above it.

This was also a great breeding ground for ducks and we saw great numbers of mallards, redheads, and scaup rising from each little backwater or eddy. The whisper of their wings blended with the screaming of terns until we scarcely noticed another sound coming in—the steady background-music of rapids in the distance.

If the rapids were really bad, there would have been a portage marked somewhere in the records. So I comforted myself as we made the approach to Deer. Soon the sound grew louder and by standing up I could see the first of the white horses. We drifted as close as we dared to the brink, spotted what looked like a good channel with a wide-open V at its throat and headed down its center. The V continued smooth and black, connected with other V's, and down went all three canoes in line. This was good water to run, plenty of depth for once, and plenty of warning, too, the tail of each V marked plainly by a spout. Down we sped with an abandon we had not known before, and the farther we went the more confident we became. This was a rapids we could enjoy. Then as before, we were in a whirlpool at its base. Not a rock had we touched, nor a drop of water shipped. We had come down as canoemen should.

Deer Rapids was good for our morale. We knew about the rocks now, the color of the Churchill, its speed and depth, the sweepers along the banks. We had survived several runs and our record had been clean, with the exception of Leaf. Perhaps what had happened there was just as well, for it had given us a hint of what could happen if we relaxed our vigilance or went down without proper reconnaissance. We needed the memory of Leaf.

One more rapids lay ahead, one final challenge before we could camp. The map said of Dipper: "Portage all the time." There were no decisions to make; we had only to find the trail. I knew Indians never carried a foot farther than they had to. If they could approach within a hairsbreadth of the lip of a chute, they would, rather than land fifty feet or a hundred above, where it was perfectly safe. I also remembered the old adage, "No Indian ever drowned on a portage." But with the river the way it was, finding a portage under a swirling torrent presented a problem.

As we neared the rapids the flow became swifter and swifter and higher over the banks and we were soon convinced that this time the portage was under water. While we were debating whether to slip into the willows or go down a little farther, I saw an old blaze on a jack pine marking the carry, but the water there was several feet deep. Portaging was out of the question and by the looks of the heavy rapids down below shooting was impossible as well. Just above the jack pine, Denis and I jumped into the water, pulled our canoe into the willows, and worked our way gradually downstream around windfalls and almost impenetrable thickets, holding on as best we could to keep from dropping completely out of sight between the boulders.

Elliot and Eric, Omond and Tony pushed inland toward

drier ground; Denis and I paralleled the river farther down. Eventually we found a brush-choked ancient trail, evidence of high water many years before, and made the carry to the other end. At one point we could see rapids and white horses such as we had never found before, great herds of them galloping in wild confusion all over the stream. No canoe could live out there for long, and I was glad we were on solid ground.

After the rapids, the marshy expanses of Dipper Lake were a relief. The river fanned out into a great delta with grassy flats and winding channels. Once more there was screaming above us, while the shorebirds and waders ran over tangled weed mats, and the pelicans coasted the horizon like little white ships. The sun shone on countless wings and the sound of calling was everywhere.

Across the marshes were cliffs and rocky islands and we would camp once more on the Shield. There were several places to choose from with ledges and glaciated shelves all along the shore. We decided on a sheltered island just across the channel from a cluster of Indian cabins on the mainland. High enough to catch the full sweep of the sunset, we would get its color over the marshes and be within sound of the moving flocks. As we neared we saw again the same orange lichens which marked our first camp site and a smooth landing place close to the water's edge. It felt good to unload the canoes that night and from our vantage point look over the country through which we had come. We stood there high above it and remembered the Drum, Leaf, Deer, and Dipper Rapids. I thought of Dr. Charles Camsell, the great geologist and explorer, reminiscing on his days in the Canadian bush.

"Of course I've known fear," he said, "but always fear laced with exhilaration."

This day, with white horses all the way from Shagwenaw, we had known fear too, and also the joy that comes when a run is over and you sit in some foam-laced eddy at a rapids' base, looking back. No one who has ever done that can forget the sight, the sound and the feel of fast water, or the wonder and half-frightened sense of triumph.

We had come sixty-five miles in three days, which seemed more like three weeks so completely had they separated us from the outside world. We took possession of our rocky island with a sense of real accomplishment and the feeling that at last we were working into the rhythm of wilderness travel, were getting the feel of the country once more and settling down to an old and familiar routine.

Camp was pitched in record time, for now each man knew exactly what he had to do. As soon as the canoes reached shore, they were unloaded, the food dumped immediately on the big tarpaulin close to where the fireplace would be. Tent packs were carried back to some level spot and deposited with sleeping bags and personal gear. Within minutes Denis and I had a fire going underneath the grate, with four pailfuls of water catching the first flames. Omond and Denis pitched the Baker, Tony the "A" Tent, Eric, his own. As soon as the tents were ready, tarps were laid down, airbeds blown up, sleeping bags laid upon them. Personal gear was placed safely inside, the canoes taken care of, extra firewood brought in by all. The voyageurs were moving with their old speed and precision. All this seldom took more than half or three quarters of an hour, and by that time the bannock was browning and Elliot and I had supper well underway. If not too late, we plunged in for a quick swim. The outfit was shaken down at last.

Omond prepared a special tot of rum that night, and we sat on the shelf and drank it while watching the sunset. A wind rose out of the east, and white caps were beginning to show on the open lake. A great white pelican floated serenely by, oblivious of the canoes and our activity. It cruised down along the shore, not more than twenty feet from the canoes and the fire.

After supper the wind grew stronger but only occasional gusts ruffled the tents. Snug in our bags, we lay listening to the gale overhead, safe and secure in a quiet pocket of the protecting granite ridge behind us. It was good to listen without having to face the force of the blow, good to lie there with rapids behind us and clear going ahead.

CHAPTER 5

REPRIEVE ON DIPPER LAKE

T wo *miles further north is the commencement of Croche Rapid, which is a succession of cascades for about three miles making a bend due south to the Lake du Primeau, whose course is various, and through islands, to the distance of about fifteen miles. The banks of this lake are low, stony, and marshy, whose grass and rushes afford shelter and food to great numbers of wild fowl. At its western extremity is Portage la Puise, from whence the river takes a meandering course, widening and contracting at intervals and is much interrupted by rapids. After a westerly course of twenty miles, it*

reaches Portage Pellet. From hence, in the course of seven miles, are three rapids, to which succeeds Shagoina Lake. . . . Then Shagoina strait and rapid lead into the Lake of Isle à la Crosse.
—ALEXANDER MACKENZIE

WHILE I WAS GETTING breakfast under way, I noticed Omond coming down from Eric's tent and wondered vaguely what he was up to. He stopped at the fireplace, stood and watched me for a while.

"Bourgeois," he said finally, "I hate to tell you this but Eric is not feeling well."

Shocked, I turned and almost upset the coffee pot.

"Nothing serious," Omond continued. "All he needs is rest and quiet. Perhaps by tomorrow he'll be all right."

The others had gathered around, concerned about the stricken voyageur.

"He is running a temperature," Omond explained, "and as long as that continues he should not be moved. His attack of flu before the trip with lack of sleep, exertion, and excitement is responsible."

It was a relief to know that it was nothing serious. Eric's durability was proverbial, and we were sure whatever his trouble, it was nothing a day's rest would not cure.

By the time breakfast was over we were in high spirits. This would give us a chance to reorganize the equipment, do some washing and cooking and savor the situation generally.

In the hurry and confusion of getting under way and during the normal routine of any expedition on the move, there had been so little time to let sights and sounds and new adventures sink in.

Most of us had traveled far. Eric, Tony, and Denis had come nearly two thousand miles from Ottawa. Elliot and Omond were on maneuvers of the Prairie Command at Dundern to the south. I had driven and flown a thousand miles from my home at Ely, Minnesota. There had been countless matters to attend to and we had all arrived at Ile à la Crosse rather breathlessly. This was a welcome reprieve and we decided to make the most of it.

No sooner had we left the fireplace than Elliot yelled: "A canoe is gone!"

We rushed to the ledge where we had placed the three canoes so carefully the night before, with their bows all pointing up hill and into the wind. There were only two. I should have taken a turn with the bow lines around a boulder or a tree, but I had been so sure that the pocket they rested in would protect them. Once I lost a canoe, years ago, and had to swim half a mile to the shore. We were in serious trouble, and the expedition was barely under way! Six men could not possibly travel through storms and rapids in our two canoes with any degree of comfort or safety.

Omond wasted no time on self-recrimination. He got out the glasses and scanned the far shore a mile away. The white-capped waves were high now and rolling across the channel. If by some chance the canoe had been blown off the ledge, it would drift over there, but in those waves it could not last long against the cliffs. He studied the shoreline, watching the spray dash high against the rocks, then steadied on a point to one side of the steepest shore. "I see something," he said. "Might be it." He handed the glasses to me.

A tiny gray shape—the canoe without a doubt—was bouncing gently against a clump of willow and birch to one side of the cliff. Up and down in the waves it moved, caught by the bushes and seemingly held there. We would have to hurry if we were to save it. Elliot, Omond, Tony, and Denis took off immediately in one canoe, and I watched as they hit the open water and all but disappeared in the troughs.

What good fortune made the canoe land against those bushes instead of the rocks we would never know. How the wind could lift it off without a sound and with no paint left anywhere was also a mystery. Not until we learned about the Mamaygwessey did we know the truth.

The voyageurs were now at the cliff, holding onto the empty canoe in the willows. For a moment they disappeared and all I could see was spray and confusion, then suddenly the two canoes broke away and were fighting the waves on the way back. It took half an hour for them to come across the channel and everyone was drenched. The stray canoe was unscratched, two of its three paddles still inside and not a drop of water had been shipped. It had drifted across the lake as lightly as a leaf. Ten feet to the north and it would have been pounded against the cliff. A little later Elliot found the third paddle floating in an eddy just below the fireplace. How it had been thrown out was also part of the mystery.

Breakfast was a time of rejoicing. With such an omen Eric was bound to be well soon and everything would be all right. There was no kidding, no sly asides at my lack of foresight. It was far too serious a matter for that, since it could have meant the difference between a pleasant and successful run down the Churchill or one constantly fraught with discomfort and danger due to overloading. We had learned that no matter what the situation, those canoes should be made fast.

Tony and Elliot decided to celebrate by catching fish. In a short time Tony, casting off the rocks with a red-and-white Daredevil, had taken thirty-two northern pike and walleyes. He let most of them go. Elliot, standing on a rocky spit above him, caught as many with a red-and-white Bass-oreno. It seemed to make little difference what they used, for the fish struck at anything that looked like food. In half an hour Tony brought me a baker's dozen of walleyes for chowder and fillets.

It seemed good to cook a meal without hurrying. I cleaned and prepared the fish and kept the fire going while absorbing the scene. When the dried potatoes and onions were simmering gently I added the fish, seasoned it with salt and pepper, added a little powdered milk and a spoonful of precious tinned butter. That, I said, was something special for Eric who needed the additional nourishment. Here was chowder as it is made in the North and as the Finns and Scandinavians have made it for centuries in Europe. No tomatoes, pork or bacon, no fancy ingredients. Just fish, potatoes, and onions, with a little something extra for good luck. Boiling fish is common in the North. The Indians boil it with a little flour, or broil oily fish like trout. Only white men resort to the frying pan.

That afternoon I made another bannock. Taking a cupful of prepared biscuit mix, I added just enough water so I could knead it into a fairly dry ball of dough. The kneading is important, for without it the bread might be too porous. Finally patting the ball into a flat cake, possibly not much more than half an inch in thickness, I pressed it into a well-greased frying pan, browned it gently on each side, then placed it beside the fire where it would catch the heat and bake slowly for half an hour. It is the traditional bread of the North, and Indians and men of the bush vie with each other in method and ingredients, and guard their recipes jealously. Some say that one must start with flour and salt and that prepared mixes are no good, others say that reflector ovens or Dutch ovens are the answer, but most of the men I know stick to the old traditional use of the frying pan.

An old-timer once told me that no bannock deserves the name that has neither raisins nor berries in the dough. Another claims that the only way to make the dough is to hollow out a place in the top of a sack of flour, add water, and knead it until it becomes a ball of the proper size and consistency. Flattened out and fried in a pan, it is food for men. Store bread is for city folks, say old-timers, bannock for the bush.

The reprieve was a pleasant break, and we would more than

make up for lost time and mileage in the extra energy generated. Our afternoon was spent in many ways. Elliot and Tony kept on fishing along the shore. Omond worked at his maps and calculations of distances covered. Denis found a spot out of the wind where he could watch the lake and catch up on his diary. I found another protected cranny from where I could see a small Indian settlement to the west. I looked it over carefully through the glasses but not a soul was around; no travelers were coming through. We were alone on Dipper Lake, alone with the clouds and the wheeling flocks of birds.

In the rush of getting started, there had been no time to sharpen my axes, so I located a round Carborundum stone and went to work. I hadn't known such leisure for a long time, and the sharpening of the two axes became the most important activity in the world. I studied several rough spots and nicks, rubbed them down with the circular motion one can use with a stone the shape of mine, first with the coarse granular side and then with the fine. As the edge took shape, I spat on the stone and finished the process gently, a few strokes on one side and then the other until the edge was sharp enough to cut a blade of grass. Our axes were single-bitted and weighed about three pounds. They each had a handle-length of 26 to 28 inches and were heavy enough for any work we had to do, from cutting windfalls or tent poles to chopping firewood or pounding stakes.

What a contrast to the little axes of voyageur days found on old camp sites and portages! They were little better than hatchets or tomahawks, and felling a tree of any size with them

77

was a major operation. Still, compared to the stone hatchets of pre-discovery days or even those made of native copper, they were a big improvement and very important in any trader's stock of goods.

I dressed the leather sheaths with oil. They had become dry and brittle and without treatment might crack and let the sharp blades through. Then I rubbed the leather until it shone and even polished the snap which tied down the closing flap. For over an hour I worked on my axes, an hour punctuated by many incidents.

A deer mouse came out from a clump of moss and paused.

"Hello," I said, "we are just a party of voyageurs about two hundred years late. One of our men has some strange malaise, which is the reason we are staying here."

The little transparent ears were spread wide, and the black eyes regarded me steadily.

"By the way," I said, "do you think your ancestors saw the Frobisher boys? They probably camped here."

There was still no movement of the eyes, though the ears trembled. Then suddenly it was gone, back into the jungle of caribou moss and rocks.

For two hundred years its forebears had picked up crumbs around the fireplaces of travelers. After we had gone, the news would spread and there would be feasting on the ledge.

Once I saw a canoe with four Indians and a dog heading across the lake toward Dipper Rapids. They saw our camp, slowed down, looked us over and went on their way. They were heading for Patuanak Village, returning no doubt from the forest fire on the other side of Primeau. Perhaps Wolverine was in the party. I could imagine the dwarf telling him at the dock that the white men had asked for him.

The pelican floated close to me, still the stately little white ship. It made its steady round along the shore and back again and I wondered how many times it had come this way, how many fish it caught enroute or whether this was simply a tour of inspection now that we were there. Mallards flew constantly overhead, and I could hear the whistle of their wings and see the sun glinting on wing bars.

Tony called several times from his fishing down the shore, and once I watched him struggle with a big northern pike, run back and forth over the rocks, only to lose it at last. He stood there ruefully contemplating his broken line. Elliot laughed and chided him, then lost one of his own.

Eric lay quietly in his bag, completely subdued, but the focus of all attention. Toward mid-afternoon, I made a kettle of tea and we sat around him like medicine men listening to Omond's diagnosis.

"If his temperature goes down to within a degree of normal we can move," he said, "but no paddling or portaging for a while."

Though we knew what his decision meant, somehow the full gravity of the situation had not struck home. It was so delightful to have a day off that none of us could take anything seriously. Not a word was said, though we could not help but wonder what would happen to our plans if Eric did not recover. A layover of several days would mean shortening the trip and all arrangements for getting out would have to be changed. Eric drank a cup of tea, pulled the sleeping bag over his head and went back to sleep. We strayed back to our various activities.

Late that afternoon Omond and I paddled over to the Indian cabins to see if anyone had returned who might know about Knee Rapids. The waves were rolling high with great troughs between them and as soon as we reached the open we fairly flew across the channel. Approaching the shore we saw that a landing might be difficult to maneuver. The only place without rocks was a slim ramp of poles with a dock of slippery logs beside it. We would have to hit it exactly right, for the dock was completely awash and the poles of peeled spruce covered with spray. A hundred yards out, coasting the four-foot combers, we made our decision. We would run straight for the ramp, jump out onto the logs of the dock and at that moment slide the canoe toward the shore. The approach had to be timed exactly right for we must hit the shore while in a trough between two crests.

We backed water as cautiously as if we were nearing the lip of a rapids, posed for a precarious instant on the top of a wave, slipped over into the trough and were hurled toward the ramp. We jumped and with one motion caught the gunwales of the canoe and slid it to safety over the poles.

"Whew!" was all Omond said. An instant later and the wave could have split the canoe on the edge of the dock or torn it on a protruding spike or stub.

No one was around the settlement, and each cabin was tightly locked. We followed a trail across the peninsula to some cabins we had seen when entering Dipper the day before. We got there just at dusk and found an old woman and several children. It was a clean little place and the dogs and children looked well-fed. The old woman was dressed neatly, her moccasins good. She tended a big iron pot hung over an open fire, and the smell was intriguing. With a chocolate bar I swiftly made friends all around. The old woman guessed we wanted to talk to the men and pointed to the landing, indicating they had just returned from the nets. We found two men and a boy down at the shore, their canoe loaded to the gunwales with suckers for the dogs. After visiting a bit and admiring their haul, we talked about the rapids below Dipper and on the way to Primeau and Knee.

"Run all of them to Primeau," said the younger man, "but watch out for Crooked Rapids beyond. That one's bad."

That seemed to be good news on the whole, but we could never be sure. What Indians said varied. To some—the good canoemen—there were few portages. To others, all rapids were bad, and usually few had traveled far from their own settlements.

The dark was settling. We hurried back along the trail with the dogs howling and straining at their chains.

"I'd hate to run into one of those critters at night," said Omond, "they're just plain unsociable."

Long before we reached the village we could hear the thunder of the waves and both of us had a vivid picture of what might happen if we didn't get away from the dock. The memory of our arrival was still fresh.

We stood on the shore and watched the rollers come in, the white, hissing crests crashing over the ramp and dock where we had landed. Why had we been so foolish? We might have to stay all night or longer if the wind kept up. Coming in was one thing, going out another. To be on the safe side I placed some matches in a dry spot beside one of the cabins. If we capsized and were washed back, we would need a fire. A long, long mile away to the west we could see a pinpoint of light glowing and sputtering. That would be Elliot making supper.

We must reverse what we had done before: Watch for one of the thirty-foot gaps between two waves, push away from the ramp at that very instant, then paddle hard to get over the next comber. This was like pushing a boat into ocean surf, the launching depended on the timing and power of the start. We stood beside the ramp while the spray dashed over us time and again. Twice we missed our cue. Then it came. We slid the canoe down the greasy poles and alongside the dock, jumped in and with a tremendous shove were free. For an instant Omond's paddle stuck between two rocks and he almost fell out trying to get it loose. Then we were fighting to reach the top of a breaking crest, hung there teetering desperately for a moment, slipped over, and were on our way.

The paddle back was exhilarating, as exciting in its way as running the rapids the day before, each wave a special problem of approach and defense. We fought waves for an hour, were blown far out of our way to the north, and finally reached our camp site only to find everyone had rolled in. Surely, I thought, they might have worried just a little, might have waited up with a fire and a cup of hot tea, but suddenly I was flattered by their confidence in our safe return.

"We could have drowned," growled Omond, "and these simple voyageurs would think it was what we had planned all along."

After a cup of tea, some cold bannock and a piece of fish, we went to bed. Tony, who had been sound asleep, muttered as I crawled in. "Bourgeois," he said, "Eric is much better."

"That's good," I answered. "Did he eat some supper?"

"Yes," said Tony, "he ate well."

The wind was still roaring overhead as I lay in my bag, and I wondered what the morning would bring. If the gale kept on, we would have some shelter from the east shore but there would be stretches where we would have to fight the waves. Even though Eric's temperature was down, he would be in no condition for heavy work. True, he might ride as a passenger and we could take turns paddling alone in the stern, but over the windswept reaches that would be impossible. Another day of delay and we would be seriously behind in our schedule.

Furthermore, we were travelers, and part of the joy to us all were the new camp sites each night, new vistas and fishing spots and the great satisfaction of having covered a certain distance on the map. Gradually all of these thoughts merged with the sound of the wind over the ridge and the uneasy lapping of the waves against the far point of the island. The canoes were tied to trees and everything was under cover.

Once during the night I waked and stepped out of the tent. The northern lights were beginning to play, but not spectacularly. The stars were bright and the moon in its quarter. It would be almost full by the time we reached Flin Flon. It was bitterly cold and the settlement was dark. I thought of waking Tony, but he was sleeping too soundly. Some other night, perhaps, when the lights were really bright.

CHAPTER 6

FATHER MORAUD

Iᴛ *is true my son," said the*
good old man, "that you will have many monsters to overcome,
and precipices to pass in this enterprise, which demands the
strength of the most robust. You do not know a word of the lan-
guage of these nations whom you are going to try and gain to
God, but courage, you will gain as many victories as combats."
Advice of Fᴀᴛʜᴇʀ Gᴀʙʀɪᴇʟ
to Fᴀᴛʜᴇʀ Hᴇɴɴᴇᴘɪɴ *on leaving*
for explorations in the west (1678)

THE MORNING DAWNED with a high wind, black scudding rain clouds and squalls that raced across the channel. I went down for a bucket of water and stood looking out over the wild and restless scene. The east was yellow and partly green, with just a rift to show where the sun should be and then it turned to gray and black. Most anything could happen.

Omond joined me. "Eric's temperature is down to normal," he said, "if he takes it easy he can travel."

"We'll break camp then," I answered, "and go as far as we can."

I prepared the usual pot of porridge, a pound of Red River cereal with half a pound of raisins, mixed a batch of fish cakes and made a pot of coffee. Eric ate with us, looking wan, but otherwise none the worse for his ordeal. I thanked him for the layover, promised in return that we would carry him over the portages, if necessary, paddle his canoe, wait upon him all day long. I knew with Eric there would be none of that.

After breakfast we loaded the canoes, skirted the point of the island, and headed into the teeth of the wind across a narrow wave-tossed channel that separated us from the east shore, then worked down the narrows toward the opening into Primeau Lake. The sky grew darker and darker and there was a spattering of rain. Swiftly we got out ponchos to cover the packs and ourselves. Then came a solid lashing wall of rain straight out of the wind, churning the surface of the lake to white. There was no escape as it bore down on us, and we

86

cringed under its impact. The packs, thanks to the ponchos, were dry, but there was now half an inch of water in the bottom of the canoes. We would soon have to land and tip them out before the packs became soaked.

Halfway down the lake the sun came out from behind a cloud. The rain stopped and there were spots of blue. The sky was still threatening but for the moment the storm was over. As we pulled off the ponchos and our rain shirts we heard the roar of a big motor from the west. A freighter canoe rounded a point of land in a plume of spray and bore down directly upon us. We could see a man standing in the bow, a tiny figure in a ski cap, with a white flowing beard and a black robe flying in the wind. When the craft was alongside our little flotilla, it stopped. We paddled close and rested in its lee.

The man was a priest. He told us his name was Moraud and that he had lived in the Churchill River country for over forty years. Denis, who spoke to him in French, discovered he was a brother of the late Senator Moraud of Ottawa and that they had many friends in common. While they chatted on and gesticulated as Frenchmen always do, I sat and studied Father Moraud.

To me he seemed the epitome of all the men of God who had braved the wilderness since the days of early exploration. A small man, hard and wiry and weather-beaten, he stood in the bow of his big canoe, a symbol of the North and of the Church. Here, I thought, might be the spirit of Father Hennepin and all the men of many sects who have given their lives for an ideal, far removed from civilization, from crowds and cities. He like all the rest had deliberately chosen a way of life different from his heritage. What he had chosen must have been adequate compensation for the loss of contact with the culture that made him what he was.

As though to prove it, on his face was written peace and a withdrawal from mundane things. He had known the North for forty years, its vast distances by canoe in the summer, by dog-team and snowshoe during the winters. The howling huskies around the villages, the long white silences and northern lights, times of starvation and disease as well as years of plenty and quiet golden autumns, all this he had known.

Beneath his black spotless robe were paint-stained dungarees. I could see them when the wind blew the cassock wide. The robe he had donned hurriedly when he came to meet us, for it was the symbol of his calling. The dungarees revealed a man of action who scorned no work. To a man of the cloth in the wilderness, menial tasks were necessary, and therefore dignified, being the work of God. He was on his way, he said, to visit someone toward Knee Lake, someone who needed help.

"Come to my cabin and stay the night," he said finally. "There is plenty room and I have food."

We thanked him but refused. We had already lost a day on Dipper Lake.

He left us then and the great canoe roared back into the waves and spray and Father Moraud stood in the bow holding onto the thwart, bouncing up and down with its pitching. The sun was out. We still needed to drain out the water, so we pushed on to a flat rock at the narrows. There we lifted out the packs, turned over the canoes, and laid out the ponchos to dry. After a pot of tea, Omond and Tony took off for Knee Lake, followed by Elliot and Eric. Denis and I busied ourselves with drying out and cleaning the cooking outfit. As we were finishing, the big canoe returned and Father Moraud repeated his invitation.

"Come and stay with me tonight," he called across the waves. "There is plenty room and food."

Again we were forced to refuse and when he saw we were determined to go on, he bowed from the waist, raised his hand in blessing and went back the way he had come.

I shall never forget that gesture from the front of that beaten-up old freight canoe. It was the bow of a courtier who understood our dilemma perfectly and though he wanted us to come, would not press the point. While we stood watching his canoe disappear in the west, we regretted our decision. He could have given us so much of the history of the country, so much of himself that we would never know. I wanted to ask how he felt about the whole Churchill River country, what was going to happen to the Indians, how they felt about the church and the precepts of Christianity and what was happening to their own spirit world. There was so much to learn that only he could tell. Most of all I wanted to know if the hardships and the life in the wilderness had satisfied him completely, if its compensations were great enough to make up for losing Quebec and Montreal and the society of those who were his cultural equals. As I stood there watching the freighter grow smaller and smaller and finally disappear behind a point, I resolved that some day I would come back, spend a week or a month with him, for it might take that long to find the answers to my questions.

But as I paddled away I knew the answers, for Father Moraud felt as Hennepin, Marquette, Allouez, and the host of men of God who since early in 1600 had followed the traders and explorers into the hinterlands. I remembered Louise Hasbrouck's description of Father Hennepin's preparation to accompany La Salle in 1678:

"Upon learning at Quebec of his being chosen to accompany La Salle, Hennepin began at once to make his preparations. These were simple since he took no other garment but that he had on, the grey robe with the rope girdle, and carried in his little bark canoe only a blanket and a rush mat for a bed, and his most precious possession, a portable chapel or box containing an altar and the requisites for saying mass, given him by one of his superiors in Canada. Frontenac, always fond of the Recollet Order dined him at the castle in Quebec, and soon after the friar, with two canoemen, set out on the first stage of his long trip. La Salle was to follow later."

The sun disappeared and the rain began again. Though we paddled off into the teeth of it, we did not leave Father Moraud, for he was with us in spirit. In the short space of a few moments sitting in the lee of his canoe we had met a man who had dedicated himself to an ancient tradition. We would never forget his bearing, the white flowing beard, the jaunty way he wore his cap, the immaculate cassock over stained dungarees. His was the spirit of all the priests who had ever gone into the bush.

"Bourgeois," said Denis, laying his paddle across the bow and turning toward me, "I wished we could have stayed."

"We should have," I said, "but now it is too late."

The rain continued, came down in sheets, and again the canoes were drenched. As we approached Crooked Rapids, a party of Indians bore down on us from the upper lake and stopped at a point ahead to make camp. They looked at us in amusement as we approached, white men paddling canoes and traveling in the rain. Surely we must be mad. What could possibly be so urgent that we must keep going in spite of the weather. We pulled alongside their overturned canoe as they came down to the shore to see what we wanted.

"What about the rapids?" I asked, but they simply shook their heads. Denis tried French with the same result. Gradually we got the impression they were not too bad, that we could run them without danger if we were careful. Our Hudson's Bay Company map said: "If the water is high as at present, go down to left of island with the canoes light. No portage. If water is low, portage on left bank." Again we would have to wait and see. No one seemed exactly sure of what to do.

Simpson met a band of Indians somewhere in this area when he came through in 1820. "Made an early start," he states in his journal, "passed through Knee Lake, made Knee Lake Portage, Decharge de Rapid Croche, and found a band of Ile à la Crosse Indians at Lac Croche, in charge of one Pellant,

A N.W. Servant. . . . Three of Mr. Clarkes Indians were in this band, they complain bitterly that they have no Company's Servant to protect them, Mr. Clarke therefore left one of his people with them, proceeded and met a Half Size Canoe from Isle à la Crosse with supplies for the Indians. The delay and neglect that has taken place in forwarding these supplies arises from the dilatory measures of Mr. Spence who was left in charge of the District for the summer. Got through Lac la Croche and Lac Primeau, made portage la Puisse and encamped at six O'Clock, Raining in torrents."

These quiet, noncommittal Indians were as much a part of the country now as then. Like the caribou and the moose they were indigenous and made little impact on the land. While as yet we had seen none of the animals, we knew they were still around. In the old days, when the caribou migrated, the Indians followed north like wolves to the barrenlands in the summertime, then south to the protecting woods during the months of cold. The great herds of caribou always moved, for only by doing so could they find subsistence. Moss and browse grow slowly in the North and could not survive being eaten constantly. Only by migration over a vast terrain was it possible for caribou to maintain themselves without depletion or exhaustion of their food supplies. So over the hills and ridges the phantom herds would drift, leaving little sign of their presence. The Indians would drift with them until they had taken what they needed and then move back to their villages along the Churchill. The wilderness returned swiftly when they had abandoned their encampments. First, grass and berry bushes, then aspen and willow would appear. And on the rocks the lichens would grow. In a few years no one would know Indians had been there.

By the time we reached the head of the lake it was late afternoon. The other canoes had stopped to give Eric a rest and to wait for us. The rain was over, but we could see no sign of a portage. With the banks in flood, old landings were out of sight, as well as brush that had been beaten down or rocks which had been marked. Denis and I moved down toward the rapids, while the others watched from their precarious positions just above the lip of the first descent. We drew closer and closer. I stood up for a final look. There was no smooth V this time, no channels down between the spouting rocks. The rapids were long and dangerous, with white spouts high and spectacular.

Realizing at the last moment that there was no safe channel anywhere ahead, we turned the canoe sharply to the left, slipped into the willows and then on into flooded birches and hung on to them with the water swirling around us. Foot by foot we pulled ourselves farther into the protection of larger trees and when the water was shallow enough, jumped out and began to wade, pulling the canoe downstream and parallel to the main flow of the river. Ignominious, but safe, it was far better than taking a chance out in the open with the dark closing in. Running strange rapids in sunlight is one thing, but doing it with lowering clouds and bad light is another. In the dusk they seem twice as dangerous.

The other canoes, seeing what we had done, went into the

willows above us, pushed farther into the shore, found an ancient trail choked with brush and windfalls and portaged down to the point where Denis and I finally came out. Drenched once more, partly from the rain, with water sloshing around in the bottom of the canoe, we knew we too would have to land soon to save the packs and their precious contents from getting any wetter than they were. The current was still fast, but we shot the balance of the rapids without difficulty and rounded a bend. There to our joy at the head of another rapids was a broad shelf of pink granite. It looked like a good camp site. We had had enough for one day, went ashore, looked it over and hailed the other canoes as they rounded the bend.

What a wild and lovely spot! The clouds were breaking up and through a rift we could see the promise of a good day tomorrow. Ducks were constantly in the air for this was a flyway between their feeding grounds. The river gurgled past the ledge, and below us were the rapids we would have to shoot in the morning. There was plenty of room for tents. The fire would be on a flat shelf close enough to the water so I could dip up what I needed without having to make a trip to the river's edge.

There was a good supply of dead spruce and jack pine and much of it was dry, in spite of the rain. In a short time we had a fire going and the tents up. Omond was at his usual ritual of concocting a potion suitable for voyageurs who had braved a storm, met Father Moraud, and come through another rapids. His mixture of rum and hot lemonade took the chill out of our bones and made us forget the long dreary stretches in the rain. There was only one toast that night: "To Father Moraud."

Tony the fisherman made a few exploratory casts along the rock and almost every effort brought a strike. In just a few minutes there were plenty of walleyes for dinner and breakfast. Swiftly I filleted six of them, and because we were white men without the Crees' taboos about frying, dropped them in the pan and let them brown. The clouds had disappeared, and the sunset was wild and beautiful. Eric was again in fine fettle, had suffered nothing, in spite of his temperature of the day before. We had run more fast water without touching the rocks, were again on schedule and well on our way in spite of our reprieve on Dipper and the bad weather.

After dinner we looked at the white water below us. It extended way down the river and the horses looked fierce and unmanageable. The center was impossible, but just across there seemed to be a smooth slick close to the bank with one sharply pointed shelf around which the water swirled and spouted. If the canoes could get past that point, they would be all right, but in avoiding it they might be drawn into the heavy waves at the center.

As we lay in our bags that night, we listened to the gurgle of water beside the tents and to the soft steady roar from down below.

"It has been a good day, Bourgeois," said Tony. "Every day is a good day and weren't we lucky about that canoe. How do you suppose it could have been blown off that rock with none of us hearing it and then landing over in those willows without a scratch? The waves going over were pretty big and you didn't see the time we had getting away from the cliff."

Before I could answer, he was breathing deeply with the rushing of the river.

"Come and stay with me tonight." That courtly bow, the brave cassocked figure bouncing up and down on the waves. Some day I'd come back and visit Father Moraud. That was something to dream about.

CHAPTER 7

THE MARSHES OF HAULTAIN

Knee Lake: *Embarked at half past two* A.M. *Got through Lac Des Souris, Lac du Serpent [Snake]. Mounted Serpent Rapids, the navigation very bad and obliged to walk up through strong brush and marshes about three miles; Gummed & breakfasted at the entrance to Lac de Sable, passed through that and Lac Croche, ascended Rivierre Croche and little Grassy River, and encamped at the entrance of this Lake at eight* P.M.

—George Simpson (*1820*)

97

The land of this lake low and well covered with Pine &c, entered the creek being part of the Mus-coo-see Se-pee or Grass River went about 5 miles from South-Westerly to East in a part not above 20 yards wide very short or rather constant turnings making about 1 mile NW through a grassey swamp, and entered the main river on the East side being about 200 yards wide with grassey, swampey sides easey current then . . . entered E-che-quan Sask-a-ha-gan or Knee Lake.

—Philip Turnor (*1790*)

THE morning was bright and clear and the rapids below looked as exciting as I had hoped. The night before they were filled with foreboding, the sound of their rushing ominous, the swirls and whirlpools deep and unfathomable. Now in the morning light all was joy and movement and they sang their ancient song of going to the sea. The crests at the lower end were silvery and sparkling, and I felt we could ride them even though the little point across the way seemed sharp as a knife.

Denis and I loaded first, pushed off into the current, and angled slightly upstream. The current was stronger than I had expected and before we were halfway over, we had to paddle hard to keep from being swept down into the rapids. We watched constantly the spout at the tip of the point. The closer we drew the more desperate it looked. That spout might hide a cutting ledge that could rip the canvas of our canoe, and what is more it might extend out just far enough to catch us as we slipped by. A hundred feet above, we nosed into the bank. While Denis held on to the willows, I jumped out, waded ashore, and found a portage that followed the river closely. The Crees evidently did not trust the point either. Just below ran a long smooth slick close to shore.

Omond and Tony followed and did exactly as we had done, joining us at the slick. But Elliot and Eric felt adventurous and took the long chance. They shot by us well outside the point and down through the billowing white water ahead. We watched them with fear and admiration; Omond shook his head. They came through without mishap and were down at the end of the rapids waiting for us before we were back on the water. Our canoe grazed a smooth boulder on the way down and began to swing. I jumped in the water, lifted it off, and we shot the rest without difficulty. All three canoes were now safely below.

"That was lovely," said Elliot. "What a beautiful ride."

I tried to look stern, but their excitement was contagious. After all, I was the only one who had touched anything. And who could argue with adventurers on a day like this?

Ahead was Knee Rapids with a three-quarter mile portage which we found without trouble. This was a real carry and well used. Because it was almost a mile in length, we used the old *posé* system of the voyageurs, carrying loads part way and returning for another before going on. Long portages are best made that way, for a man can rest going back. And breaking a long carry is always more pleasant than trying to do it in one stretch. The canoes now weighed at least a hundred pounds and while that is not too much of a load, to men who do not make a business of packing, it is enough. In my younger days I used to take such a canoe and a pack totaling possibly one hundred and fifty pounds or more, and I knew the others had done it as well. But we had all discovered that as time is of no consequence or heroics either, such effort had little to recommend it. Furthermore, using the *posé* system gave us a chance to visit. Separated as we were in three canoes, it was always pleasant to get together on a trail.

If the packs were heavy we took only one. If light, we doubled so that each man carried the same weight, plus extra paddles, rods or other gear. Inasmuch as each canoe had three or four packs, this usually meant making two complete trips. We alternated carrying the canoes over each portage, irrespective of length. The long Knee Rapids portage was Denis' turn.

"My canoe," he said wryly, testing the tightness of the yoke screws and lifting the craft to his thigh. "As I recall, Bourgeois, the last portage was about twenty yards. There is no justice on the Churchill."

He tossed the canoe on his shoulders with an easy flip and trotted off down the trail.

It was interesting to watch the ground for signs of game and halfway across the portage we found the track of a big moose, the hoofs as large as those of a cow. The prints went straight down the trail and I carefully avoided stepping on them. As yet we had seen no moose, which was not surprising along such a major route. Indians traveling up and down would soon kill off any animals on the portages or along the shores. Perhaps if we were careful we might see this one feeding in a bay.

A squirrel chattered from the branch of a jack pine and I stopped for a moment to look at it. It was the little pine squirrel of the Quetico country, with white-rimmed eyes and a black stripe along the flank, and it chirred incessantly and stamped its feet.

At the first rest Tony said: "Bourgeois, did you see the moose tracks?"

"A big one," I said. "Might go fifteen hundred pounds by the way he sank into the trail."

On the way back we studied the tracks and noticed how the animal had browsed a twenty-foot birch by rearing up on its hind legs and riding it to earth to get at the tender branches of the top. A number of trees along the trail had been bent, broken, and mutilated. I could not help but think of what would have happened had we been a party of Crees packing across that portage.

Killing a moose was always a great event for the Indians and reason for rejoicing. No other creature had such fine meat or a more valuable hide. The caribou did not compare in flavor or nourishment and moccasins or mittens made out of moosehide were more precious than gold. Furthermore, a moose was large enough to feed several families for days, and no part was ever wasted. No opportunity was ever passed up for securing one, so I decided this one was just plain lucky.

At the end of the portage we saw that second Knee Rapids

would be easy—a good smooth slick with no uncertain spouts. We pushed in and shot through without difficulty into Knee Lake.

A southwest wind had come up—exactly the opposite direction from the wind that had almost pinned us down on Dipper and Primeau. It was warm, and packs and clothes dried swiftly. Off came shirts and we reveled in the sun as we coasted with the breeze down the lake to Bentley Bay. We had earned the respite and it was good medicine for Eric not to have to push so hard for a few hours. On the northeast side we saw a cluster of Indian cabins, Elak Dase settlement according to our map, with the white spire of another of Father Moraud's missions. We passed within a hundred yards, skirted the sandy shore and the snarling huskies, pushed on into the landing. Before one of the cabins were four Indians; two old women, an old man, and a girl in her teens who was very shy. They looked at the ground all the time we were there, but smiled when we gave them cigarettes. They love cigarettes and would rather have them than candy. We took pictures and visited, though they spoke neither English nor French very well. They knew nothing about the next rapids, but did tell us the church was Father Moraud's and that he had just finished painting the steps and had cleaned the inside. Perhaps that accounted for the stained dungarees. We walked past a tent, some fish-smoking racks, and more dogs.

Each dog had his own little hole in the sand; each one was chained and ugly. As we walked by, they bared their teeth and snarled. A fish a day or one every two or three days was enough to keep them alive but not enough to keep them happy. Gaunt and mangy, by the looks of them they hadn't been fed even that often and had they been lose might have torn each other to bits.

There was a tiny garden with some turnips trying bravely to hold their own. The church was very clean, the hymnbooks worn. They were printed in Cree, as was the catechism. As I thumbed through them I wondered how much the natives understood. But this much was sure, to them Father Moraud was a symbol of goodness.

While we were down at the landing, two women came in with a small birchbark canoe. A moose hide was in the bottom and on it a basket of Saskatoon berries. It was a welcome sight to see them paddling and making use of the craft their forebears had known. One of the women indicated they were short of food and we gave them what we could spare.

We were now in the estuary of the Haultain, a winding marshy river coming down from the north. The shores were low again with little evidence of the Shield, much like the country approaching Dipper Lake. Each time a river joined forces with the Churchill there was a delta of wide and marshy flats. The Haultain was no exception and, as usual, I began to wonder if this would be our night for a camp in the willows, if for once our luck would run out. There were great weed mats and thousand of gulls and terns. How they soared in the sunshine, some of them snow-white with black wing tips, some of them dusky, wheeling and dipping and constantly screaming. Great flocks of yellowlegs, snipes, and sandpipers skittered and ran everywhere.

"Swarm of bees," commented Denis.

Again there was the impression of the entire country being in flood, as though not only the water was flowing but the land as well. Even in the marshes there was a perceptible current, moving, always moving toward the east, the grasses swaying like grain fields in the wind. Blue sky, blue water, and white soaring wings against them, but more than all else, the constant sound of calling birds.

Around each bend I hoped to see some higher ground, but nowhere was there a rock or ledge, only a continuation of the low marshy shores. Toward mid-afternoon we approached Dreger Lake and there the shoreline began to take shape. While there was only the slightest hint of firmness in the banks, I could almost sense the coming of the headlands. Toward the end of the day we rounded a final bend and directly before us was a high smooth promontory. The canoes sped toward it, but as we pulled in at its base we saw that the slope ran straight up from the water's edge without a level place anywhere. I could not resist, however, the invitation of the long, smooth expanse of rocky slope before us, so I jumped out and ran over the silvery gray caribou moss to its very top. There, out of breath and trembling from exertion, I stopped. A magnificent vista of water and forest lay before and behind me—the marshes of Haultain. This was the Lonely Land. More than ever from that height the flooded country seemed to be moving. Flocks of terns and gulls glittered in the level rays of the afternoon sun, sometimes silver and sometimes tinted with red and orange. What a wild high picture it was! In my joy I almost forgot the purpose of my climb.

Back at the canoes, I reported we would have to look further, but in the meantime Omond and Tony had discovered a low flat shelf of rock directly above where we had landed.

"Come over, Bourgeois," called Tony. "You will like this place."

Over I went and it was a perfect camp site, with a broad flat shelf running like a dock along the water with depth enough to unload the canoes right there. Back of the landing were level places and abundant firewood. Once more we were in luck.

I laid out the pots and pans and food supplies on a ledge polished by glacial ice, built the fireplace close to the water where I could dip up what I needed, set the dishes out to one side on another little shelf, for all the world like a table. Never before had I known such luxury.

"Are you happy, Bourgeois?" asked Denis.

I did not answer but bustled about as contentedly as a house-wife in a modern kitchen. It was late when we finished supper, and we sat there for a while after everything was stowed away. There was firewood for breakfast from a dead jack pine—kindling from its resinous roots, with a handful of birch-bark tucked under my canoe. The tents were pitched, the beds made, nothing to do but sit and look. We heard motors coming down the lake from the east. In the dusk about a hundred yards out in the river were three large canoes heading for the settlement just above. One of the canoes veered and then swung into our camp. We went down to the stone dock and warped the craft alongside. In it were two grandparents, a son and his wife, and a little girl named Caroline.

The Indians were in a gay mood, for they had killed a big black bear on the last portage; the bloody carcass lay among the gas cans in the bottom of the canoe. I remembered the remark of one of the old women at Elak Dase that they were in need of food, especially meat. What a homecoming there would be! The stew kettle would go on immediately and there would be feasting and rejoicing far into the night. How happy they were and how typical it was of all Indians on the move.

But little Caroline intrigued us most. Not more than seven, perhaps, and shy as a fawn, she snuggled down between the two older people. She had big brown eyes, good features; she smiled at me and for that got herself a cookie. The people said she belonged to a family down below, but had decided she wanted to go visiting with them and stay for a while. This is typical of the Cree attitude toward children; they are always taken care of, whether they have a family or not. Caroline, the young woman told me, might stay with them for several months or all winter if she wished, and I knew she would be as welcome there as at home with her own people.

After half an hour they left and roared up the open river on the trail of the other canoes. It was then that Omond told the story of the Eskimo he and Elliot had visited the year before when they were inspecting Dew Line sites. It was in the Hecla and Fury Straits region along the northwest coast of Hudson Bay.

"We had stopped at the village of Igloolik," said Omond, "and one night under a bright full moon we were awakened by laughing and yelling. Looking out we saw that the entire village of some two hundred men, women, and children, was playing tag on the ice and having a wonderful time. We wouldn't have been quite so surprised, if it hadn't been 2:30 in the morning."

"Remember," said Elliot, "the day we were out in the big boat and I looked at my watch to see if it was time for lunch, and how the Eskimo laughed?"

"You asked them," continued Elliot, "what was so terribly funny and one of them answered, 'White man eat by clock, Eskimo eat when hungry.'"

Those stories are typical of the way of life of all primitive people, wherever they may be—their feeling of timelessness, their joy in play and doing simple things. Only we are constantly worried about time, schedules, and the seriousness of life; only we are apt to forget that life can be fun. Those Indians going up the lake, in spite of the fact they were no doubt hungry and the people at Elak Dase more so, still had time for visiting and getting the most out of the happy adventure that was theirs. Children, perhaps, but as we listened to the fading drone of their motor far up the river and thought of the feast waiting for them and little Caroline's easy shift from one situation to another, I wondered if we did not have much to learn.

We were now at the lower end of Dreger Lake with the marshy estuary of the Haultain well behind us. In the morning we would work into Sandy Lake, then into the valley of the Snake, skirt the northern fringe of that huge body of water and camp somewhere near Belanger village below the mouth of the river of that name. One thing that had begun to impress us was the number of Indians along this famous route, concentrated around the missions and the Hudson's Bay Company posts. There were far more Indians than ever before and certainly more than the country could support through hunting, fishing, and trapping.

What complicated the problem was that they no longer traveled widely. They preferred to stay close to their established bases, instead of following the dwindling caribou herds into the tundras of the north. Handicapped by motors, the need of gas and oil and heavier canoes, few of them undertook the difficult and almost impossible long trips into the hinterlands with families. No longer did entire groups move several hundred miles to secure supplies of meat and skins. Lone hunters or trappers might contact the animals occasionally but bringing back sufficient quantities for the stay-at-homes was out of the question. Furthermore, the number of caribou had dropped alarmingly, even in the remotest regions. Whether due to disease, destruction of feeding grounds by fire, or in some instances overshooting with high-powered rifles, the great herds were no longer the basic source of supply they once had been to the Crees, the Chippewyans, and other tribes of the Northwest.

CHAPTER 8

THE VALLEY OF THE SNAKE

T HEN *follows the Lake des Souris* [Sand Fly], *the direction across which is amongst islands, northwest by west six miles. In this traverse is an island, which is remarkable for a very large stone, in the form of a bear, on which the natives have painted the head and snout of that animal; and here they also were formerly accustomed to offer sacrifices. This lake is separated only by a narrow strait from the Lake du Serpent, which runs north-northwest, seven miles to a narrow channel, that connects it with another lake bearing the same name, and running the same course for eleven miles, when the rapid of the same denomination is entered on the west side of the lake. It is to be remarked here, that for about three or four miles on the north-west side of this lake, there is an high bank of clay and sand, clothed with cypress trees, a circumstance which is not observable on any lakes hitherto mentioned, as they are bounded particularly on the north by black and grey rocks. It may also be considered as a most extraordinary circumstance, that the Chipewyans go north-west from hence to the barren grounds, which are their own country, without the assistance of canoes; as it is well known that in every other part which has been described, from Cumberland House, the country is broken on either side of the direction to a great extent; so that a traveller could not go at right angles with any of the waters already mentioned, without meeting with others in every eight or ten miles.*

—ALEXANDER MACKENZIE

TONY AND I were up shortly after dawn, and before the others had waked we climbed to the top of the hill. The marshes lay covered with mist; the eastern horizon was mother-of-pearl and rose. From that height, it seemed to us that the river ran in all directions, as though there was more water than land. The land itself appeared saturated, trembling, unstable and slipping downstream. Gone were the sounds of wings and the calling. There would be silence for another hour.

"You should have seen it yesterday," I said.

Back at the tents all was activity. Omond had started the fire and Elliot had the pots boiling merrily and the coffee made. By the time breakfast was over the outfit was ready to move. Never shall I forget the glory of our start down Dreger Lake. The sun was shining brightly and the country had been washed by the rains. Birds were calling again, pelicans soaring against the blue. The terns and the marshes were still with us, and flocks of ducks constantly passed overhead. In the air was a feeling of exaltation, exactly why I do not know, possibly because of the knowledge we were through with the lowlands, wet weather, and the uncertainty of the river and its rapids. The fact we had survived all this and passed some sort of a divide was no doubt responsible for our elation.

I believe too, it was the realization that from here on we would see more of the Shield. Great marshes, while they are enjoyable for a time or when seen from the heights, can be depressing if one is in them too long. In spite of the birds and their calling, in spite of the sense of flowing the country gave us, one thought was always in our minds: Will we find a high place to camp? I have been in many marshy areas and know what they mean. I have enjoyed them to the fullest, but I would not choose them for any length of time. Perhaps this comes from having lived in high rocky country most of my life. Mountain men feel the same way. Until they are high enough to look over the surrounding terrain, they are out of their element and vaguely unhappy.

At the end of Dreger we came to a short rapids where the Churchill River, compressed into a narrow defile, demonstrated its power and ferocity. The rapids were wild and impassable with a huge boiling wave in their very center. One look was enough; it would be suicidal to attempt it. Brush beaten down at the water's edge marked the portage, so we knew the Indians had never taken a chance. We unloaded and made the carry, but we were fascinated by the great swirl and returned and stood there wondering what it would do to a canoe. Almost like a pin wheel, the swirl was no doubt caused by some tremendous fissure underneath which spewed the current upward. A canoe hitting it on either side would turn over. If it hit head on, it would go straight into the air and over backwards. In my travels I had encountered pin-wheel spouts, but never a monster such as this.

On Sandy Lake, which we entered now, we looked in vain for beaches until halfway down, where we stopped for lunch. This beach must have given the lake its name but like many names had no real meaning, for it was the only sand we saw. The valley of the Snake coming up was no doubt in the same category. With few reptiles in the entire country, seeing a snake would be an event. Some early traveler must have been so impressed on finding a small garter snake that he gave the area its name. Sometimes canoemen do strange and un-explainable things such as naming a chain of lakes in the Quetico region This Man's Lake, That Man's Lake, The Other Man's Lake, and No Man's Lake, all in a neat row.

I thought of all this as we walked up and down the beach at our lunch site. A bear had walked the full length of it the night before. Its tracks were still plain, except near the water where the ground was less firm. At one end a wolf had jumped out on a rock near the water's edge. I could picture a great timber wolf, cousin to all the sled dogs along the waterway, standing there poised and alert looking out over the lake.

Near our lunch spot was the track of a mink. Two by two the delicate footprints wound in and out of the sedge and among the rocks, where he had investigated anything that might mean food. Ravens had hopped along the sand and sandpipers had danced, weaving and running with the flow as they did on all beaches.

All creatures seem to appreciate the freedom and space a beach provides. It gives them a chance to escape the entanglement of vegetation. They can find food in the warm shallows —crustacea, worms, insects, and mollusks for the waders; fish for the bears, the wolves, and ravens; windrows of seeds for upland birds; and always something alive and unaware for weasels and mink. This sand beach was important in the ecology of the Snake Valley.

After lunch we paddled toward Snake Rapids, the outlet of the lake. Just above the drop, we went ashore looking for the portage. Trees were criscrossed everywhere, still as hard and brittle as the time they went down in a burn some years before. In many places it was impossible to walk on the ground and one had to jump from log to log in order to make any headway at all. A slip, and down you would go into a jackstraw tangle of sharp and splintered spruce. If you should damage your canoe in such country and have to go out on foot, it would not be easy.

The family who had visited us the night before had indicated that there were no real portages between Dreger and the

Snake. By keeping to the left we could run all fast water without difficulty. According to the map there was a long portage possibly two miles in length on the left, but we saw no sign of it. Perhaps the Indians were right this time.

We got into the canoes, studied the rapids once more from the top, saw that the left-hand channel was smooth and fast. It skirted the heavy white water in the center, where waves seemed to be three to four feet high. One final look and we started down. All went well until we rounded a bend and were confronted by a roar and a spray that blocked our way. There was no channel in sight. An island loomed in the very center of the confusion and we headed for its closest point and landed in a swirl.

We pulled the canoe out of danger and waited for the rest. They might need help if they did not hit the point head on. Omond and Tony bore down next, paddling madly to avoid being swept to one side. I grabbed their bow and held it while they jumped into the water. In an instant the canoe was on the shore and the packs thrown helter-skelter up out of the way. Eric and Elliot now hove into view around the bend. For once they had lost their nonchalance after seeing the island and the tumbling white water on either side of it. I waved and they came straight toward us, hit the shallows and made the landing in a furor.

Elliot looked over the situation. "Well," he said grinning, "imagine meeting you all here."

Omond was already scrambling down the spine of the island. "Looks like an old portage," he yelled.

The Crees sometimes made sport of danger, or so it seemed to me at the time. Instead of cutting a portage around, they preferred to take a chance and hit the point of an island laced on both sides by impassable rapids. If they, or we, had missed that point, there would have been trouble.

"In low water," said Eric, "it wouldn't be so bad. Remember, the Churchill's in flood. Three feet higher than normal."

It was here I snagged myself on one of Denis' lures. It had hung by one of its gang hooks on the gunwale of our canoe after the last fishing, and while we both knew it was there and could have rescued it a dozen times, we neglected it. When I picked up the canoe on the portage, the lure caught in my trousers, the sharp point of one of the hooks easing its way into my skin. I knew that if I moved or dropped the canoe, or tried to throw it on my shoulders, the hook would be forced deeper into my stern than it was, possibly even beyond the barb itself. The others had gone ahead, and I stood there helplessly wondering what to do. I tried to sit down but each time the point warned me. I attempted to ease the canoe back to the ground, with the same result. I was trapped by one of those impossibly ridiculous situations that are fun to remember but unadulterated misery at the time.

I finally solved the problem by reaching back with one hand while I balanced the canoe on my thigh with the other and with a courage born of desperation, gave the lure a quick jerk, tearing it loose. When Denis returned a few moments later, he looked at me questioningly, wondering at my delay.

I handed him the red-and-white Daredevil spoon without comment.

"Thought we had lost it," he said.

"You almost did," I replied, "and your Bourgeois, too."

The little portage was rocky and once I slipped and fell going down a smooth wet slope with a canoe on my back. The rapids roared on either side and when we got to the end, we found still more heavy water and surging foam-laced currents. We loaded the canoes, tied in the packs, and coasted down the remainder of the rapids without mishap. We turned as we hit the quiet waters of MacDonald Bay and looked back. What a conglomeration of ledges and boulders made up the bed of that rapids! It was frightening to see them and to realize what could have happened had we not been lucky enough to hit the point of the island.

This was big country, built on a grand scale. The Snake itself was thirty-six miles in length, and the bay we were now traversing was fifteen miles across. We would skirt only the north side of the lake, see little of its tremendous reaches to the south. But even the part we saw was impressive: great rolling ridges with broad valleys in between them, huge expanses of burns grown back to aspen and birch, but in many places, stands of climax spruce stiffly pinnacled and dark against the sky.

In this country, due to carelessness, fires have been a scourge for thousands of years. Somehow in the midst of such vastness, the burns seemed as natural ecologically as the old stands themselves. As I looked over one of its far vistas, the country appeared to be in a constant state of successional change, from the healing of the scars after fires to the gradual invasion of deciduous trees and conifers. I climbed a hill during the afternoon to get a broader view. All around as far as I could see were the various stages, first the purplish glow of fireweed, then the light green of aspen and birch, the slightly darker green of their maturity intermixed with spruce and jack pine, finally the stands of solid spruce. So it will always be until men change their ways in the bush.

Early travelers spoke often of fire and how they sometimes lost their way due to smoke.

"We are obliged to anchor our canoes by a small island, instead of unloading them, as is customary every nite, for the whole country is on fire. Whether by accident or design, I know not. . . . Our people who pass this way every summer, say that, almost every year fire runs over this part of the country which is then of course nearly destitute of animals."
—Daniel Harmon (*1800*)

"The natives are frequently very careless in putting out fires they make, and a high wind kindles it among the Pines always ready to catch fire; and burn until stopped by some large swamp or lake; which makes many miles of country appear very unsightly, and destroy many animals and birds, especially grouse who do not appear to know how to save themselves but all this devastation is nothing to the Indian; his country is large."
—David Thompson (*1796*)

Even then I knew lightning would play its part as a major ecological force no matter how conscientious men became in putting out fires. There would still be conflagrations due to this cause alone. Everything had adapted itself to this constant change and were the pattern to vary greatly, life in the north would change as well. Burns mean new growth for mammals and predators who prey upon them. Although caribou depend largely on mosses and lichens, they also need browse. Fire, controlling the growth of browse, influences their numbers as well as migration. Primitive man was dependent on the larger herbivores and his migrations followed theirs.

Going through the narrows between MacDonald Bay and the main body of the Snake, we saw our first Indian pictographs high on the rocks to our left. They were in the same maroon pigment in which they occur in the Quetico-Superior country and for that matter all over the world. According to experts, the color is usually a combination of fish oil or animal fat and an oxide of iron—hematite for maroon, magnetite for black, limonite for yellow. No Indians know their age or exactly what they mean, but we are sure that they are primitive man's first attempt to set down in pigment the records of his hunting, his dreams, his legends, and his spiritual beliefs. We did not climb the slope to examine them because it was late and we were tired, but one figure was plainly visible —a small round-headed creature with no nose and long spindly arms and legs with six fingers and six toes. Had we known that this was the only place on the river where pictographs showed some variety, we would have stopped in spite of the thirty-seven miles of river and open lake we had traveled—a good stretch anywhere in the north.

We headed out into the open water of the bay and toward some islands. There at the west end of Cowpack Island we found what we were looking for—a site with a sweeping view of the lake and a violent sunset. A thunderstorm was building around it and the loons were calling madly. As we cooked supper and made our tents fast against a possible blow, I could not help wondering what would happen in the morning.

Philip Turnor must have tried the fishing on the Snake when he came through in 1792. His diary reads as follows:

"June 13th Wednesday, at 4½ AM took up the nets got a few fish and at 6¼ AM got under way, stoped 1½ hour at the head of the Snake fall being much wind afterward we went to the lower end of the Snake River and out at 8¼ PM and set our nets. Wind and weather as of yesterday."

We had no net to set, but Elliot and Tony went to work and in a few minutes had half a dozen northern pike and some walleyes. They released the northerns and filleted the walleyes for breakfast. Turnor must have camped somewhere nearby after coming down the Snake; he could have set his nets at the end of the last rapids or in a narrows between the islands.

I gathered a lot of fine kindling—ends of spruce and balsam dead and dried in the wind, some shavings from an old resinous root and shreds of birchbark—and stowed the bundle under the big tarp that protected the food. Then I anchored the edges with big stones. We snubbed the canoes tight to the trees, tested the tent ropes until they sang with the tension. We were facing a gale and if it should break, we might be in for trouble.

A soft moaning was in the wind and a feeling of wetness—no mist as yet, but a certain something in the air that warned of what was to come.

Old-timers and Indians have this sort of sixth sense about the weather, a sense above and beyond barometers, something learned through a hundred thousand years or more of watching the skies. Dormant among those who have lived too long in cities with shelters impervious to storms, it can become alive and reliable with experience. It isn't a case of feeling arthritic aches or pains, but a physiological response as definite as the reaction of a barometer to pressure and humidity, and in its way fairly accurate, provided of course neither reason nor logic is allowed any influence.

I left the shore and crawled into my bag beside Tony. "What of the night?" he asked. "Will it storm?"

"It cannot storm," I answered; "the tents are in the teeth of it."

"Goodnight, Bourgeois," he said, "sleep well."

When we arrived, we had been too tired to look any further for a camp site, and there was the chance that storm would pass us by. But as I lay in my bag I was convinced that something was on the way. I wished that we had picked another spot.

CHAPTER 9

SANDFLY TO BEAR

Embarked *at day break, got through the lake* [Black Bear Island], *made Portages Canot Tournier, Bouleau and arrived at Portges. des Epingles at ten* A.M. *where we found Messrs. Oxley & Andries, also the N.W. Brigade detained by strong adverse wind, our Brigade came up at two* P.M. *Gobin one of the Bowsmen was nearly killed on the last Portage by falling under the canoe. Being anxious that Messrs. Oxley & Andries should accompany us, gave them a man out of my canoe: Mr. Clarke agreed to do the same, and take a keg of rum from them in order to lighten their canoe, but he afterwards changed his mind, kept the man, and returned the Keg, after filling his liquor case out of it; these gentlemen must therefore follow. Mr. Robertson was nearly drowned in the Rapid of this Portage when taken out a prisoner by the N.W. last year; it is a dangerous rapid, and I suspect his persecutors intended that it should have been his grave; two of the Crew were lost and his escape was miraculous. The weather moderated at four* P.M. *when we embarked, passed through Lac des Epingles* [Sandfly], *and at eight* P.M. *encamped at the Entry of this lake.*

—GEORGE SIMPSON (*1820*)

I CAME TO with a start just before daybreak. It was raining hard, the mosquito bar blown in, and the ends of our sleeping bags soaking wet. A pool of water an inch deep extended far into the tent. My hunch had been right, for the storm had come with a vengeance and done everything expected of it. I looked over at Tony and decided not to wake him. No one could travel in such a gale, and we might as well wait. There was no sound from the other tents, but the big fly of the Baker was whipping madly in the wind. The rain was drenching them, too.

Only the end of my bag was wet. I pulled it in as far as I could, listened a moment longer, and went back to sleep. Instead of four thirty, I awoke at six thirty. The rain was over and the wind down. I retrieved the kindling and dry wood from under the canoe and started a fire, cooked a big breakfast—bacon and fish, the very last of our precious eggs, and a bannock with raisins. Long ago I had discovered that if voyageurs are to be happy on stormy mornings they must eat well. A full stomach gives courage and cheer, which are far more important at such times than strength.

I smiled when I thought of what a party of voyageurs would have done, how they always took off rain or shine at dawn or before, paddled for several hours before they even thought of breakfast and then feasted on their inevitable gruel of peas or corn and a little fat. Frances Simpson's records of early morning starts are classics:

"May 3, 1830—Arose at 2 A.M. with aching bones occasioned by the dampness and hardness of my couch. We then travelled till nine o'clock and breakfasted at 'Point Original.' Everything was calm and quiet, not a sound to be heard excepting the stroke of the paddle and the clear mellow voice of our principle vocalist Tomma Felix, singing *La Belle Rosier* and other sweet voyageur aires."

We had become too accustomed to comfort and must be well-fed before taking off. We should remember how real men of the bush had traveled in the days of the trade. Breakfast tasted good and in spite of the rain we were all in good spirits. We rolled the wet tents, packed our gear, got under way and all but sailed down the upper reaches of the Snake toward a spot marked on the map as Belanger. Soon the wind shifted and within an hour cleared the skies of every cloud. With the sun out the storm was forgotten. The country was washed and lush once more and mist hung in the valleys. Just before noon we noticed an encampment of Indians on a point ahead. There seemed to be a good many men, women, and children, all down at the shore waiting for us to come in. With the wind behind us we landed in a grand flurry on smooth shelving rocks and with the help of many hands, canoes and their precious cargoes were pulled out of danger. Possibly twenty in all, the Indians had come up from the settlement down below to cut wild hay for a horse and a few cows they owned. There was an older man in charge. Most of them were boys and girls. Jovial and friendly, they posed for pictures, and the little ones smiled at our gifts of candy.

I was impressed with the happy, carefree air of the group. They had come to work it was true, and eventually it would get done, but there was plenty of time to do it and visit with us too, plenty of time to sit on the rocks and watch for half an hour as we came in and then again until we were out of sight. Improvident, you might say, but I wonder what would have happened had they been working for a wage. The lack of a price incentive made the difference; with no paycheck in the offing, the work of getting in the hay was a happy holiday instead of drudgery. So it was with hunting and fishing expeditions when the objective was getting food for everyone and there was no thought of compensation beyond a fair share of whatever was taken. Whites know the feeling when working on some community project, be it a barn raising, getting in the crops of a neighbor in need, or building a common stone wall. As soon as time is bought, the attitude changes.

We asked the boys about Needle Rapids coming up at the outlet of Sandfly Lake, but no one seemed to know anything. Once more I was impressed by the inability of the Indians to give any real advice. They were familiar with the country, but felt no particular need to remember intimate details of terrain. Rapids and portages were not important because they knew them well, nor were landmarks, except where they pointed the way. This I understood, for not long ago someone had asked me to give some accurate information about my home country the Quetico-Superior where I had packed and portaged many thousands of miles and knew the land as thoroughly as the Crees knew theirs. When pinned down, I was abashed to discover there were many little things I did not know. On the scene, I seemed to know instinctively where to go, but away from it the entire country was a grand, misty blur of portages, camp sites, fast water, timbered ridges, and countless lakes. And so it was, no doubt, with the Indians. While they do not travel as extensively as they once did and in many areas have given up long hunting, fishing, and trapping expeditions, they know terrain without being able to describe it.

Regarding Needle Rapids, some of them said, "Go right side," and some, "Go left." About Snake Rapids of the day before some said, "Take two mile portage," others, "Run rapids on the right." None even mentioned the little island in the center over which we had finally portaged. Part of the reason may have been that they traveled in large canoes and did not look at the water from the standpoint of small, sixteen-foot Peterboroughs. What they could do with their enormous craft was entirely different. As a result, we never pressed them for advice and when it was given, took it for what we thought it might be worth.

As we passed through a marshy stretch beyond the mouth of Belanger River, three boys in a motor canoe passed close by. They swung toward us and held up some big fish taken out of a net and the carcass of a deer they had shot. They did not stop, but like boys, wanted to impress us with their prowess. Haymaking was only part of the day's activity for them; there was always variety, something to lighten drudgery. Why they were going to the village just then was anyone's guess. Perhaps they wanted to pick up some tea or to deliver the fish and venison. They should have stayed with the haying for they were big and strong. One could have gone instead of three. Two went along for the ride.

Sandfly was a beautiful lake, by far the most beautiful we had seen so far—good timber all around it, most of it mature spruce, many smooth glaciated islands and channels and countless good camp sites. As we wove our way through the maze we envied the Crees with time to burn and no schedules to keep, time to fish and explore for a few days and really get to know the country.

Sandfly. What a strange name for such a charming body of water! It was christened no doubt during May or early June when the flies are bad. We paddled along with our shirts off, enjoying the feel of the warm sun after the drenching of the night before, and didn't see one fly all the way down.

This lake was similar to those of the Quetico-Superior. Until this point I had been making comparisons. "The Churchill is too big," I would say to myself; "it is too swampy, too gale-swept and too much in flood to live with happily. The Quetico country has more charm, more intimacy, and poetry." But now that feeling was dispelled. If the present formation had continued for a hundred miles, with some stands of pine to break the continuity of spruce, I could have imagined I was at home.

Just after leaving Sandfly, and still coasting with the wind, we approached Needle Rapids and Falls. We knew there must be a portage, but from that distance we were not exactly sure of its location. As we neared the outlet, the place where the shoreline dipped, we saw that the river split itself into two channels with a falls or drop in each. The problem was to pick the right one and riding the crest of the combers I knew there would be little time to decide when we arrived. We were now within a hundred yards of the outlet, but still no landing was in sight, only big, round boulders with waves crashing over them. No matter which channel we chose, we would have to maneuver quickly to keep the canoes from swamping or cracking up.

It seemed that the best chance lay on the left. A huge wave nearly hurled us into a melee of boulders and white water. Then above the drop we jumped into the water, hauled the canoe to safety, and stood there on a flat ledge leaning against the gale, breathing heavily, somewhat abashed at what we had done. In a moment Eric and Elliot hit the water just in time and hauled their canoe out of the waves beside us. Omond and Tony were nowhere to be seen; evidently they had chosen the channel to their right.

Those great waves, how beautiful they were! We stood at the drop of Needle Rapids watching the green and white combers marching down the full length of Sandfly and feeling the sting of their spray. This was the north at its best, the sort of thing that more than compensates for any grief. We had known the feeling many times—when marooned on some spit of rock with the wind doing its best to blow us off, when sitting below a wild rapids with the shouting all behind us, or at the end of a day with adventures to remember. It is then that an expedition means the most; for a moment life had been seasoned with excitement.

The portage was a very short one, perhaps not more than a hundred yards. Poles had been laid over its entire length to keep the big freighters from being scratched by the rocks when dragged across. We scorned such convenience, tossed on our canoes as usual, and hurdled the poles to the other end.

The wind was still behind us and we bore north-northeast toward the far tip of Blackbear Island Lake and the mouth of the Foster River. In such a gale we might make five or even six miles an hour, and we all but flew down the open channel. Late that afternoon, we pitched our camp at the east end of the lake, exactly one week and one hundred and sixty-five miles from our start at Ile à la Crosse. We were on a little island, on a perfectly smooth rock with just enough space for the tents and a fire. We would have the morning sun, compensation for the loss of a sunset. And our outfit could dry after the deluge of the night before.

We had covered a third of the route, had spent a week learning something of the Churchill, its people and its moods, and what was very important, we were now well organized. I knew without looking where every bit of food and equipment was located, and there was no need to rummage through several packs to find a particular item. The work had become so routine that there was no question as to what should be done and by whom. During that first week every man had found his own particular niche and performed his task without question. When we made camp, there was no lost movement, no waiting around. It might have seemed like a lot of pointless scurrying to anyone watching—packs being moved, wood, tent poles, and stakes being cut, equipment strewn all over the site—but within an hour after landing, the tents were up, beds made, supper under way, and everything stored neatly away for the night. Order could not have come out of such seeming chaos without organization.

I had been chosen as cook partly because I like to cook and perhaps because I labored under the illusion I could throw a meal together faster than anyone else. No one argued the point, and Elliot, who was just as good, contented himself with being my helper or cookee. I have never seen a faster man in that all-important capacity. He could all but read my mind and because he was an excellent cook himself, would constantly anticipate and find things for me before I asked for them. We were a good team.

As soon as we reached a camp site, Denis collected rocks to support the grate. So expert had he become that when his canoe reached shore he all but leaped for specimens he had spotted before landing. By the time the cooking packs were undone and their contents dumped on a tarpaulin, he had the stones in position and ready for the fire. Then he looked around for dry kindling and wood. Finally he helped Omond with the big tent.

Eric swiftly pitched his little pup tent and helped the rest of us with ours, cutting poles and stakes and gathering stones to hold down the sides. When everything was ready, he retired to select readings appropriate for that night from the explorers' diaries.

Tony put up the two-man tent which he shared with me. When this was done, the air beds inflated, sleeping bags laid down, and our personal equipment dried and placed inside, he caught some fish no matter where we were camped, found extra firewood for breakfast, and did various tasks.

Perhaps the most important job of all was Omond's, for each night he prepared our ration of rum for the long-awaited moment when we would get together to talk over the events of the day. These were joyous occasions and all day long we looked forward to them. We had mixtures of dehydrated fruit juices, oxo, chocolate, and Kool-Aid, with some of the most fantastic flavors and color combinations imaginable. But it was always different, and never once did he disappoint us. By the time the pots were boiling, the tents made up, and a swim out of the way, something was always ready. To sit on the rocks with the smell of woodsmoke and supper in the air with nothing to do but look out over the water or listen to Eric read from the explorers' diaries was a completely satisfying experience.

It was good just to sit there. Occasionally someone would remember a happening of the day, something to laugh at, but most of the time we sat quietly, our thoughts not going much further than the contents of the blackened pots simmering over the fire.

That night on Black Bear Island Lake, I said to Omond: "Thought we lost you when you decided to pick the right-hand channel at Needle Rapids."

He was sipping his rum and studying the horizon.

"Our canoe was the only one that did it right," he said reprovingly. "And did you happen to notice we were waiting for you down at the beach, watching you hurdle those poles after barely getting out alive from the surf over those boulders?"

Somehow that had never occurred to the rest of us, but it was the truth. They had picked the proper channel, after all.

"Your bag is pretty wet, Bourgeois," said Tony. "I hung it in a tree to dry."

I went over to the fireplace, stirred the pots and tasted their contents. The bannock was browned to a turn, with just the right amount of crispness around the edges, and the stew was nearly ready.

CHAPTER 10

SILENT RAPIDS

FROM *thence a rapid river leads to Portage de Hallier, which is followed by Lake de L'Isle d'Ours* [Black Bear Island Lake]: *it is, however, improperly called a lake, as it contains frequent impediments amongst its islands, from rapids. There is a very dangerous one about the center of it, which is named the Rapid qui ne parle point, or that never speaks, from its silent whirlpool-motion. In some of the whirlpools, the suction is so powerful, that they are carefully avoided. At some distance from the silent rapid is a narrow strait, where the Indians have painted red figures on the face of the rock, and where it was their custom formerly to make an offering of some of the articles which they had with them, in their way to and from Churchill.*

—ALEXANDER MACKENZIE

133

SUNDAY MORNING was quiet, sunny, and warm. A benediction lay over the land, and the furor of travel and violent activity seemed far behind us. This I felt must be a different sort of day. Though we must move on as usual, we would do so with dignity and without hurry. It was a good way to feel, and I sensed that I was not alone, for the others were going about their tasks with a deliberateness we had not known since our start at Ile à la Crosse.

The smooth rock lay in the full glow of the sun, and we spread out sleeping bags, tents, everything wet by the storm. The food was spread on ponchos so every bit of mold would get the benefit of the warmth. Bacon was hung high on the branch of a tree where the sun could reach it from all sides. While breakfast cooked, I walked slowly around and around, turning each precious item so that all parts would dry.

Breakfast was eaten leisurely; there was none of the bustle that usually accompanied breaking camp. I noticed that for once the packs were not down at the shore, ready for the canoes, but I said nothing, knowing the spell that was upon us. We ate quietly, watching the water and basking in the sun.

I felt this was a time for something special, so I pulled out my wallet and thumbed through the dog-eared clippings I carried to read when held up by wind or rain. They were soiled and torn, for they had been wet many times, but the thoughts they held were as clean and hard as when they were written. I selected an excerpt from an article by Dr. Edmund

W. Sinnot of Yale, looked it over, and remembering long discussions of the past when stormbound on forgotten lakes, began to read.

"Is there evidence of plan or purpose in the universe? I find it hard to imagine how such a universe was created without assuming there is something in it like a mind. Order suggests purpose. As Sir James Jeans put it, 'The universe begins to look more like a great thought than a machine.' "

I stole a look at the voyageurs. They were listening, but their thoughts were far away from the world of ideas.

"There is a realm inaccessible to the intellect," I continued, "and to our senses alone. In this realm open to the insight of the spirit . . . we have a sure support for that morality and good will which are necessary for human society."

Denis was throwing tiny pebbles into the water, first far out, then closer, until the spreading circles made a chain of ripples at his feet. Omond studied the sole of his boot with growing concentration. Eric looked calmly at the horizon. The warm sunlight, the blue sky and water, the soaring gulls, were evidence enough of plan and purpose and mind, and if they were not, what difference could it make on a morning such as this?

I tucked the little clipping back into the wallet without another word. Later on perhaps, when we were paddling down the lake, I might take it out again and read it. Then I would have miles of distance and unbroken hours to think it over.

The packs were clean and dry now, much lighter than when we had landed. It was a pleasure to toss them into the canoes, knowing their contents were no longer soggy and likely to mold. When we were loaded, I strolled over the site, checking each place where we had been, found an empty tin, a bit of string, some aluminum foil, a square of paper. I shoved these treasures into the bottom of the can with a stone on top for burial in deep water. Soon the caribou moss would cover places where it had been scuffed off the rocks. Only the blackened stones of the fireplace would show where we had stopped for the night.

Omond checked the map and laid out a general course bearing southeast.

"Over there to the east," he said, pointing with a stick toward the upper end of Black Bear Island Lake, "is Silent Rapids. If Mackenzie was right, we'll have to watch ourselves."

When Eric had finished his reading the night before, we had been thoughtful and apprehensive, especially at the part where Mackenzie had mentioned appeasing the evil spirits with offerings. Indians didn't do that without reason. But now as we stood there looking down the lake, the rapids did not seem so desperate. Silent Rapids—even the sound of the name fitted into the Sunday mood of us all. As we paddled away toward the east and our rendezvous with the dreaded whirlpools, none of us was very concerned. Nothing could happen on a day like this.

An hour later, when we stopped for a pipe, Tony said: "It is easy to understand Sir James Jeans out here, is it not, Bourgeois? Even Silent Rapids is part of it all."

"Yes," I replied, "it is always easy in the bush. Everything is simple, and on a morning like this even the rapids cannot be too impossible."

"That is right," he answered. "I know that it is true."

As we pushed on, I thought of what he had said. On Black Bear Island Lake where we had only to enjoy ourselves, such conclusions were logical and self-evident. The lake was beautiful, the shores and islands glowing with light. We were in good health and spirits, and there were no dangers ahead we could not overcome. It was enough to be alive.

As we neared the narrows of the lake, however, I became increasingly aware of what lay ahead. Just as with the Drum, the sound of the name began to grow in significance. There was no portage marked on the map, no information about any sort of trail. All who knew anything about Silent Rapids had talked with an evasiveness that was not exactly conducive to peace of mind.

Somewhere between those closing shores and before they opened up again was Silent Rapids with its suction and its whirlpools, and below it the pictographs where the Indians had made their offerings. Gone now were the comforts of philosophy and the long thoughts that had been mine in coming down the lake. Once again I had the feeling I had known at the Drum, the Leaf, and on the Snake. We approached cautiously, ready to head into the willows if necessary. The current quickened and the canoes gained speed. There was no roar this time, no white horses, just a soft chuckle and swish and the growing sense of the river becoming alive.

Its quietness filled me with foreboding. If we could have seen spouts and waves we would have known what to do, but how does one prepare to cope with what is unseen?

As we neared the brink of the drop-off, I stood up and looked ahead. There was only smooth swift water with foam-laced swirls beginning to show. Surely, I thought, we can go through no matter what the currents are. I looked once more as the canoe began to settle into its run, then raised my hand. The others came on.

Faster and faster we sped toward the famous whirlpools. We gained more speed and were sweeping through powerful crosscurrents. In that moment in spite of all I could do, the canoe began to swing sideways, almost at right angles to the current.

"Paddle!" I yelled to Denis, and his great shoulders all but lifted the canoe out of the water. We straightened out and shot down across the great swirl. Once again we were caught in a series of crosscurrents that almost turned us around before we regained control. By now, however, all fear was gone and I knew we would make it. I remembered then that Mackenzie had forced his way up against the current lining and poling, an entirely different problem from going down with the stream. I looked swiftly behind me. Eric and Elliot were weaving around as we had done but had the advantage of having watched us. Tony and Omond were coming straight down behind us. Then suddenly we were all at the rapids' base, in quiet water. Silent Rapids was behind us, and we sat in the main channel somewhat deflated, looking back at what should have been a frightening experience.

"Pretty rough," said Eric. "We should have portaged."

Shortly afterward we saw the Indian paintings Mackenzie had mentioned and sat there wondering about them, imagining the birchbarks of the past and the preparations for going up against the current. As usual the pictographs were on a flat vertical rock surface. There were figures of animals and birds, and strange hieroglyphics whose meaning we could only guess. This was one of the few places where such pictures were considered important enough to be mentioned in a diary.

Black Bear Island Lake has three possible routes into the main body of water, all of which looked equally good. We decided on the middle course as being the most traveled and the best. Helped now by the strong current coming through the narrows and by a southeast wind, we made excellent time. A magnificent body of water, the lake was about twenty miles long and so full of islands and channels that it was often difficult to see the mainland. The shores were high and rocky and covered with jack pine and spruce. The valleys were filled with birch and aspen, a welcome change from some of the burns we had passed through a few days before. As far as I could see, there had been no bad fires for many years.

Again the quiet descended. Silent Rapids was past, and over the land was the peace and sense of leisure of the morning. Then I remembered what I had planned back at the camp site, so I took out the clipping I had read and a passage I had copied out of Dostoevski. I tucked them both against the pack before me where I could read them over and over and think about them as they deserved.

The universe begins to look more like a great thought than a machine.

I looked over the wilderness of islands and rocky shores, the slopes of pine and spruce with broad valleys in between, and thought of man's conquests in outer space and the meaning of the new universe he is discovering. Somehow it did not seem as important as what I saw before me.

Then I read the excerpt from *The Brothers Karamazov* in which the old monk advises his followers:

"Love all God's creation, the whole and every grain of sand in it. Love every leaf, every ray of God's light. Love the animals, love the plants, love everything. If you love everything you will perceive the divine mystery in things."

There was no difference between his thought and that of Sir James Jeans, for what they both found was the same. Here before me on Black Bear Island Lake was all life, here the great thought, here the order of the universe and the divine mystery. I need look no further.

We spent the entire afternoon traversing the northeast end of the lake. As we moved onward, our canoes became a part of the great panorama of islands and channels and of the thoughts I had lived with since our start that morning. Toward late afternoon, the wind died completely and we drifted to a little spruce-grown island about five miles from the portage into Trout. Here we would camp. I placed the little clippings carefully back in my wallet and pushed into shore.

The island evidently had never been camped on before, since it was necessary to hack out spaces for the tents from an almost solid wall of spruce and balsam which covered it. Tony chopped out a square room near the fireplace and was delighted with his work until he noticed that the ground cover, a deep bed of sphagnum moss, was so saturated with moisture that it would be like sleeping on a wet sponge. He cut off boughs from the trees he had chopped and laid them over the moss and on top of that put a tarpaulin. When he had finished, he called me.

"Look, Bourgeois," he said, "never before have we had such luxury."

I left the fire and went over to admire his work. The tent smelled of spruce and sphagnum, and that with a foot of boughs on top gave us a bed such as we had never had before. The Baker tent went up behind ours in another room carved out of the same wall of spruce. It was a tiny camp, but a delightful one, and there was a flat rock beside the water's edge. That alone made me happy, for with such a kitchen a camp site is always good; places for tents can be found anywhere. Of course, at times the tents are a long way off and often without vistas and hidden from the water. Still, it does not matter too much, for once pitched, there are only two considerations, food and a place to sit and visit a while before turning in.

After supper we sat on our rock and looked out over the

lake. There was no real sunset, although the sky was angry with violent purples and streaks of yellow that might mean anything in the morning. It was good to be on an island again, for they have a special appeal. No matter how small they are, there is always a sense of remoteness like the feeling one has on a ship at sea.

Ours was a very special island, for it had escaped the fires of the mainland for many years. The heavy stand of spruce and the lush bed of sphagnum proved that. Nothing had changed very much here for a century or more, and its ecology had reached a stage of permanence rare in a land where fire could be expected periodically. Even though the shores appeared relatively untouched by recent burns, there were few places like this. On this tiny pinnacle of hard, resistant rock that had survived millions of years of erosion, time had had little effect.

Ahead of us were many islands, so many in fact that the horizon looked like a continuous shore. There were tiny ones no larger than rafts, slivers of rock like the backs of surfacing whales, crooked ones with little beaches tucked into their bays, large ones with high cliffs and stands of spruce. In among them, you could lose yourself quickly, for there were intricate little channels that led to hidden places no one had ever seen. As we sat on our own little spit of rock, we shared their charm and solitude.

The sky was growing dark. What little sunset there had been was now completely gone, and the wind was beginning to rise. It was time to get the outfit under cover. Our canoes were pushed far into the wall of spruce and lashed tightly against the coming storm. We piled extra rocks over the tarp that covered the food packs in case there was a blow.

As I lay in my bag listening to the soft moaning of the wind, I was full of the day and its adventures, its sense of benediction in the morning, the long leisurely paddle down the lake, Silent Rapids as we went through the narrows, and now the peace of our island camp hewn out of the spruces.

Elliot and Omond were tightening the ropes of their tent. They tried one of them and it sang like a taut wire.

"That ought to do it," said Omond as he twanged another rope.

"De win she blow on Lac St. Claire," recited Denis from inside the tent, "She blow dan blow sam more. Eef you don' drown on dees beeg lac, you better kip close to sho'."

Finally there was no sound and the camp was asleep. The water chuckled against the rocks, washed and washed against the ledge a few feet from where we lay.

"Bourgeois," said Tony turning toward me, "Mackenzie went upstream, did he not?"

"Yes," I said. "Remember the offering place was below the rapids, not above. We must try lining up sometime. We might find out that he was right about the suction of those whirlpools.

CHAPTER 11

TROUT LAKE FALLS

S TARTED *at four* A.M.—*made
Descharge des Ecors, Petit Roche, La Trout and Portage la Trout,
where we found the Brigade. The canoes are in a very leaky
state, and no gum to repair them; I requested Mr. Clarke to furnish the Brigade with that article as they passed Ile à la Crosse
which with great reluctance he agreed to do, provided Lamallice
chooses to humble himself and ask it as a particular favor. I however told him it was the duty of the Gentlemen in charge of Ile à
la Crosse to provide such articles for the use of the Brigade and*

that the Company's business must not be neglected even if the Guides manners were not so courteous as he could wish. Gave the people a dram and proceeded, made Portage de Aurice and encamped on an Island in the middle of this lake at eight P.M. Blowing hard and very cold. Mr. Clarke ahead.

—GEORGE SIMPSON (*1820*)

THE MORNING dawned gray, with a southeaster, a radical change from the favoring winds we had enjoyed almost every day since the start of the trip. There were no waves as yet; the surface was merely rough enough to make us work. We headed directly into the breeze, across an open stretch toward another narrows.

The discharge here was fast and smooth, no rocks in sight, no swirls or crosscurrents, just deep, swiftly moving water. It was as if the lake had concentrated its entire volume in this little narrows and had gouged out enough of a channel so there was little turbulence. Denis lifted his paddle and smiled.

"This," he said, "is the proper way to run a rapids. This we can do with dignity." He laid his paddle across the bow and leaned back against a pack.

Down we went straight as an arrow, though the wind was strong enough to blow waves back upstream. At its end we were spewed into the labyrinth of islands and channels we had seen from our camp the night before. For some time we maneuvered through them, escaping the short violent gusts that made travel in the open so slow and difficult.

Again the lake narrowed as we neared Birch Rapids. Eric and Elliot found a portage on the right side close to the river, the rest of us one on the left. We soon saw, however, that there was more fast water to run beyond the end of the portage. I walked over to a little promontory and looked it over. There was smooth, fast water, a few riffles, but plenty of opportunity to maneuver. We would run them as smoothly as before.

Such places were pleasant to shoot, for by now we had overcome our fears and had become accustomed to fast water. We knew how the river behaved around obstructions. Little rapids like these could be played with. If anything happened, we could hop out into shallow water and guide the canoes, no matter what the bottom might be.

Trout Lake was long, winding, and beautiful. In spite of a cross wind, we made steady progress. Toward noon the sky began to clear, and as the sun came out and the water sparkled, our spirits rose. With the exception of Leaf Rapids at the beginning of the trip, none of the canoes had even touched a rock or a ledge. As we made our way down the lake that morning, we were happy and confident. Even fighting waves seemed good.

We ducked into a little protected channel to have lunch and found a small flat rock just large enough to get out on. It was almost like sitting on a raft flush with the water. Our lunch was the usual one—a pail of lemonade from our supply of crystals with enough sugar to taste, hard summer sausage, Cheddar cheese, hardtack with butter and jam, a handful of raisins and a bit of chocolate for dessert, enough to keep us going until suppertime.

Weary after the morning's pull, we stretched out on the rock for a nap—all except Tony who could not resist the opportunity to fish. Soon, however, he too was out like the rest. Those breaks after the midday snack were rejuvenating. If we did not sleep, we lay and watched the sky and listened to the birds. Never more than half an hour, it was something we all looked forward to. It also gave us a chance to check our bearings, look over the maps again and iron out any questions of navigation that might arise. Elliot and Omond, the navigators, took charge of these sessions, augmenting them with shorter consultations en route. Seldom did their calculations fail, and so dependent had we become upon their judgment, we never argued with them for long.

After lunch we paddled several hours toward the north outlet and then had to decide whether to choose the route into Crew Lake or take off to the north. The northern passage somehow seemed better. Just why is hard to explain. A combination of influences backed by long experience with maps and the vagaries of wind, weather, and terrain usually help make the decision. Sometimes a choice is wrong, but if a man follows his hunches and does not argue, his decision usually will be sound. It proved to be right this time, and in the late afternoon we came to the little-used portage around Trout Lake Falls. It was a pretty trail skirting the brink and ending just below where the water was still covered with foam and the air full of the sound of falling water.

Out in the open we turned and saw the falls in its entirety

for the first time. Omond and Eric took pictures even though the light was bad. Half a mile below, we found our camp site, a smooth rocky shelf above a new rapids with the falls in full view, white water below, and the valley full of the sound of them.

"Like a picture postcard," said Elliot. "Even the coloring."

The tinting of the sunset was almost too perfect to be true. We stood there in amazement.

"Looks to me," said Eric, "more like one of the conventional sketches by early Canadian artists of the voyageur's country." He thumbed swiftly through his journal. "Listen to what Philip Turnor said when he came through in 1790:

'Went SW to W ½ mile on south shore of an Island strong current and led around a bad point on the Island dangerous of forcing the canoes side in against the rock, the current turning so very sudden, entered a part about ½ mile wide went WNW 1½ mile and came to a fall carried 120 yards over a rock on south side went S W ¼ mile and came to a fall carried on South side 150 yards not good carrying, put up at 6 PM. Wind westerly heavy gale, Lat 55° 41′ 5″.' "

"He must have camped just above the falls," said Omond, checking his map. "He'd be out of the wind up there and all set to come up Trout the next day."

"He didn't notice how pretty it was," said Elliot; "just anxious to get off the river and make camp."

Again we were on a rock beside a river. The water swirled deeply just off the ledge, all indications of wonderful fishing. I asked Tony and Elliot to catch enough for supper as soon as the fire was under way and the tents up. Omond soon joined them and the first strike was his. A tremendous pike broke water—all of three feet in length and broad across the back. It fought in the current, coming to the surface time and again, then bore down into the depths and headed out into the open river only to come charging back toward the landing.

While watching, I heard a shout from Elliot: "I've got a monster, too!" And sure enough not twenty feet away he was fighting another just as large. He ran down the shore to get away from Omond's line, the two of them far too involved to notice that Tony just above them was in the same predicament, also having hooked one of the huge great northerns for which this country is famous. All camp activity came to a stop as we watched three fish being landed at the same time, each determined to break tackle in the swift current of the river.

Omond's came in first, a pike over twenty pounds, then within minutes Elliot's, and finally Tony's. We laid the three fish on the rocks. They totaled sixty-odd pounds. We admired them, delivered the *coup de grâce* with a beaver stick waiting by the fireplace, then wondered what to do with them. It was too late for pictures and too much to eat at one time, so I decided to clean them at once, use what we could for supper and breakfast and smoke the rest to carry along for lunch snacks during the next few days.

What beautiful fillets they were—golden yellow in color, about twenty-four inches in length, four inches wide and an inch to an inch and a half in thickness. The frying pan was waiting and after rolling two of the steaks in flour, I dropped them into the hot bacon fat. Elliot mixed a batch of mashed potatoes, and we ate until we could hold no more.

With what was left of the fried fillets, I stirred up enough fish cakes for breakfast, using the old recipe of fish, mashed potatoes, dehydrated onions, a dash of flour to hold them together, and some powdered egg for color and flavoring. Twelve cakes were placed in a pan to wait for dawn.

Then I went to work on the remaining four fillets, cleaned them thoroughly, rubbed them down with salt, pepper and bacon fat, and laid them on the grate over a smoldering fire made of peeled sticks from an old beaver house. No spruce or pine went into the smoking fire, only the cleanest of birch or aspen, thoroughly dried and cured. The fillets quickly turned to a golden brown and I tended them carefully, knowing that for days ahead we would have something other than sausage and cheese for lunch.

We could have caught a dozen pike had we wished, for the waters between the falls and the rapids were alive with minnows. I am sure we could have taken several hundred pounds. Samuel Hearne in his early journal mentioned the size of the pike. "Pike," he said, "also grow to an incredible size in this water, and I have seen some that weighed upwards of forty pounds."

The three we had taken were large, but I knew they could be even larger. One recorded in the Quetico region was well over forty pounds.

Long after my friends had rolled in, I sat before the fire tending the big steaks. It was a satisfying task. The preparation of food always is satisfying on the trail. I nibbled the edge of one of them, salted them again slightly and basted them with bacon grease. Trout need no basting, for they are fat in themselves, but these fillets of the big northern pike or jackfish as they are called all over Canada, are proverbially lean and dry.

The night was clear, the stars bright, no bird calls, no loons or huskies, no sound but the rushing of water. Around me the great silence once more. It was good to sit there watching the slow fire and listen. This was still the old north, the Lonely Land, but I wondered how long it would remain, with Canada's industrial expansion on the way and the burgeoning population increase, not only in the United States, but within Canada herself.

This was the soft underbelly of the last great wilderness on the continent. I could see the civilization to the south lying against it like a hungry young animal probing, pushing, exploring, milking the untouched resources above, and as it fed, making its growth felt. Like all feeding young, bursting with vitality, it must gorge itself with the sustenance there for the taking. Already there was talk of a road from Lac la Ronge, another to Ile à la Crosse, and one to Athabasca to tap the unexploited country to the north—the oil and the minerals with which it is blessed.

Wilderness had come to be a precious thing to us and to many thousands and I wondered how it would be if people no longer had any knowledge of wild country or any opportunity to know what voyageurs had known.

The falls were fading now in the dusk, but I could hear them more plainly than ever, music that had not changed in thousands of years. Then it seemed as if there was a different note, a certain somberness that had not been there before. As I listened, I could hear still another sound, an obligato to the rest, an exuberance and a pulsing-with-life as it always is on the frontiers of the world.

I turned the steaks once more. They were all an even, golden brown now and their flavor about right. I put on a few more small sticks, banked them with ashes so they would not flame, moved the grate a little higher, then went into the tent. As I lay in my bag I could hear the singing of the rapids, with the deep roar of the falls as a steady undertone, and I lay there half asleep listening to a symphony with many shades of meaning.

According to Omond we were 208 miles along our course —almost halfway to our goal. Ahead was the Lake of the Dead. I wondered about it and the story that would surely come when Eric read from the diary again. It was hard to imagine any great tragedy in such a peaceful land, but I knew what disease could do to native tribes, as well as starvation and bitter winters when gales howled out of the Arctic and the mercury dropped to fifty or sixty below zero. These summer months were the easy ones on the Churchill.

There was a flicker of light from the fireplace. Evidently one of the sticks of aspen was burning too brightly. I went out of the tent and covered the wood with ashes once more. Tony waked and joined me and we sat in the soft glow of the embers.

"It has been a good day," he said. "One of the best. And wasn't that something having three pike on at the same time?

You know, some nights I almost hate to go to sleep for fear I shall miss something, so when I found you were not in your bag, I came out."

I cut off a sliver of the smoked fish, handed it to him and he sat munching it before the fire.

He smacked his lips. "Better than smoked sturgeon," he said, "better than caviar from the Caspian."

I cut off another sliver for myself, and it was very good. We had about ten or twelve pounds to carry with us and could have smoked enough to last us the rest of the trip, but there would be fish everywhere and a fresh smoking was always best.

Before we went back into the tent, I once more stoked the fire very carefully. We carried the three great heads and the skins and entrails to a little point of rock just below camp. Gulls would find them in the morning and clean up swiftly. Their calling and screaming would wake us at dawn.

CHAPTER 12

LAKE OF THE DEAD

T̶HERE *is then a succession of small lakes, rapids, and falls, producing the Portage des Ecors, Portage du Galet, and Portage des Morts, the whole comprehending a distance of six miles, to the lake of the latter name. On the left side is a point covered with human bones, the relics of the small pox; which circumstance gave the Portage and the lake this melancholy denomination . . .*

Since the small pox ravaged these parts, there have been but few inhabitants; these are the Knisteneaux tribe, and do not exceed thirty men.

—ALEXANDER MACKENZIE

THE FIRST RAYS of the sun came over the far ridge and touched the top of the falls. The plunging spray sparkled with light. The light shone on the sea of mist over the river and its whiteness boiled and fumed. The valley was full of the sound of rushing water. A flock of mallards whispered by overhead on their way to some feeding ground above Trout Portage.

I loosened the ax from where I had left it in a log and walked over to a dead tree that had some good, dry branches. When I raised the ax I became more conscious than ever of the quiet, and I could not bear the thought of what a shattering blow would do. The voyageurs should sleep another half hour. Nothing must disturb the spell that lay over the river. I walked back to the fireplace, laid down the ax, gathered an armful of squaw wood, sticks, a handful of pine needles, and shreds of bark from the ground to start a fire. When the tinder burst into flame, I carefully laid the wood on, went to the water's edge, filled the pots and put them to boil.

The falls were blazing now and the sun was burning the mist off the rapids. By the time breakfast was ready, the river would be clear.

The smoked fish was done, the long brown fillets cold and stiff. I cut off a fine sliver and munched it with satisfaction as I nursed the fire. The fish was good and salted just right. I hung the fillets in a bush nearby where they might catch a little more of the smoke before being packed away.

A pinch of salt went into the porridge pot. As the water

came to a rolling boil, I added two cupfuls of raisins, and the meal. I put the pot at the edge of the grate where it would simmer until done, and the pail of boiling coffee in the ashes to steep.

"Good morning," said Tony.

I was startled. So engrossed was I with the cooking, the scene before me, and the little tasks of getting breakfast ready, I had not heard him stir or come out of the tent.

"What a spot we have found," he said, "and such fishing." He went over to the fillets and stroked their long smooth surfaces fondly.

I poured a cup of coffee for him and gave him a slice of smoked pike.

He sat down beside the fire and stared into the flames.

"Where to, today?" he asked.

"Dead Lake," I replied, "unless the wind stops us."

"Dead Lake," he repeated, and took a bite of smoked pike. "What a bad name in such beautiful country."

I recalled Mackenzie's diary and the explanation given there.

"But that was long ago," he said, "and the Indians have come back. What worries me now is this talk of roads and the opening up of all this country."

"I've been thinking of that, too," I answered. It reminded me of what Hemingway said in *Green Hills of Africa:*

"A continent ages quickly once we come. The natives live in harmony with it. But the foreigner destroys, cuts down the trees, drains the water, so that the water supply is altered and in a short time the soil, once the sod is turned under, is cropped out and, next, it starts to blow away as it has blown away in every old country and as I had seen it start to blow in Canada. The earth gets tired of being exploited. A country wears out quickly unless man puts back in it all his residue and that of all his beasts. When he quits using beasts and uses machines, the earth defeats him quickly. The machine can't reproduce, nor does it fertilize the soil, and it eats what he cannot raise. A country was made to be as we found it. We are the intruders and after we are dead we may have ruined it but it will still be there and we don't know what the next changes are. I suppose they all end up like Mongolia."

The mist was all gone from the river now and the rapids sparkled and sang. They were still young as the land was young. We were there to enjoy it, and the great machines seemed far away. For a brief time we had been living in harmony with the land and, like the Crees, we made no great changes in the terrain.

We had flown in to our starting point at Ile à la Crosse and would fly out again at the end of the trip, so we were dependent on machines and would go back to a life dominated by them. This we could not change. It was part of our lives, but being able to return to the old simplicities and to live for a time in a land the machines had not reached was a privilege none of us discounted.

"Bourgeois," said Tony, "it is time for breakfast," and sure enough the voyageurs were abroad and packing. It was so easy to sit there thinking and listening to the sound of the water that work was almost forgotten. Denis was singing at the top of his voice, and Eric, as usual, was splashing around in the icy water. Omond and Elliot were coming down with packs on their backs.

While we ate our fish cakes we studied the rapids below. Seldom did we have such a chance; there was usually time for only a quick look from one vantage point.

"I think," said Omond over his coffee, "that the channel to the left is best. The high white crest in the center goes well down the channel."

"That looks good to me," said Elliot, "but we'll have to keep well away from the middle. That white stuff means trouble."

"From the standpoint of the navy," spoke Denis, reaching for another cake, "I'm for keeping all craft away from reefs and shallows. That white crest all the way down is like a string of buoys in mid-channel."

"We can't quarrel with the navy," said Eric.

We cleaned up the dishes, stowed away the cooking gear, brought down the canoes and loaded them once more. It was a good morning for shooting, bright enough to take the ominous quality out of any stretch of fast water. According to the map we would have a number of rapids to run before nightfall, but at the moment nothing seemed difficult.

Elliot and Eric led off. In spite of their resolve, they went a little too close to the crests of the main channel, got sucked into the edge of the waves, bounced around wildly, and at one point were almost turned across the current. We watched with interest, decided to stay as far to the left as possible, without hitting the rocks near shore. We followed a smooth slick within a few yards of the bank and came through without even approaching the billows in the center. When we reached Elliot and Eric, they looked a little sheepish, but no one said a word. They had received their lashing on the way down.

Of the six remaining rapids between Trout and the Lake of the Dead, we portaged two and ran four. The second was more exciting than all the rest, heavy water showing below, the result of the current boiling up against the calm water at its base. From the top of this run, the upsurge did not look serious, but when we hit the waves they were almost more than the canoes could manage. There is something unpredictable about such a backwash and a canoe in the midst of it is sometimes hard to control. When we saw what was coming, we did the only logical thing and bent to our paddles, coasting over the tops of the waves at full speed. Had we been slow those waves might have upset us.

After the canoes were together again, Denis and I discovered we were the ones who had caused concern.

"For a while," chided Eric, "we couldn't see the gunwales of your canoe, just two black figures bounding around in the spray."

Denis looked at me with surprise. "Bourgeois," he said, "I thought we had done rather well. Your voyageurs are becoming critical. No Bourgeois of the old brigades would have tolerated such insubordination." He shook his head dolefully. "We must watch them; this must not grow into an open incident."

When we reached Dead Lake the wind was beginning to rise.

We stood on the lee shore in a protected little bay. It was perfectly calm. But out in the open, whitecaps were dancing. Overhead and above the tops of the trees we could hear the wind, a steady roar, and we realized that this was no summer-afternoon breeze, but a full-sized gale. There was a decision to make, whether to coast the rollers to the eastern shore or play safe and be windbound where we were. By running with them, we could possible make the far shore in an hour and a half. If we chose to stay we might have to wait until evening or the next day.

Omond consulted his map. "Six miles across," he said. "We should be able to duck into some islands as soon as we cross the open stretch."

There was no real danger and we were confident we could ride the blow. I took a vote; everyone was for it. A long point stuck out from the north. We would have to quarter the waves to skirt it or run a chance of being dashed against the rocks. That would take navigating. Should a landing be forced, we would surely be windbound, for it would be impossible to launch the canoes again with the waves pounding in. Our Peterboroughs were in for a testing.

We checked the trim of each canoe and paddled out into the open. For a quarter of a mile we felt only the softest breeze, but just beyond we began to feel the full force of the wind. Within a mile, the fury of a powerful blow was behind us and we were riding great rollers with tremendous speed. Running with the waves is a challenge, each one a problem. There is no chance to look back and one can only feel the lift of them. A bad move with the paddle and the canoe might turn sideways and ship water. At first we were far too busy to think about anyone but ourselves, but as we got into the swing and rhythm of riding the rollers, I stole a swift glance over my shoulder to see how the others were faring.

At times the canoes all but disappeared in the troughs. What was more spectacular than anything else was to watch a canoe climb to the top of a crest, hang there for a moment as though unsure that it would make it over the top, and then crash down into the trough ahead. It wasn't really as dangerous as it looked however, for our canoe was doing exactly the same and we weren't shipping a drop, but the perspective from the side was far from reassuring.

I studied Omond and Tony's canoe, about two hundred yards away and even with ours. Each time a wave came from behind it seemed as though the gunwales were awash, but miraculously it lifted high to slip smoothly over the crest and down into the trough. A comber broke and caught me in the middle of my back. It was ice-cold. I flinched and began to quarter more sharply toward the end of the point.

The others were quartering now for the same reason. We had to make that sharp promontory or we would be forced to land in a flurry of water-soaked gear. We could see the spray hitting the rocks, and did not dare get too close. In spite of all we could do, however, the wind kept forcing us toward them, and the end of the point seemed more impossible to reach than ever. We were now running in the smooth troughs of the waves, for only by doing so could we hope to complete our maneuver successfully.

The point was now within a few hundred yards and we could see its sharp tip with the spray dashing high above it. Then suddenly we were slipping past, not a hundred feet away. Like flyers in formation, we turned and ducked into the protection of the lee and rested there watching the combers march by outside. That was a joyful reunion, sitting there in the calm and listening to the roar overhead.

"Wow!" said Denis. "I've been in some big stuff but nothing as personal as this. Those things look mighty different from a bridge. That was too close for comfort."

Elliot laughed as he always did. "Good fun," he said.

Omond was concentrating on his map. "We can have lunch down the lake somewhere in one of the channels out of the wind. We must have made that six-mile crossing in about an hour."

I wondered as we sat there if the point we had rounded was the one Mackenzie mentioned in his diary.

"It was on the left side coming upstream," explained Eric. "It could have been that one or one of those we passed on the way."

After our rest we headed toward the northeast, found a quiet place in the lee of an island, boiled a pot of tea, and ate some smoked fish and hardtack. While we lay stretched out in the sun, Eric read to us from David Thompson's diary:

"From the best information this disease was caught by the

Chipaways (the Forest Indians) and the Sieux (of the Plains) about the same time, in the year 1780, by attacking some families of white people who had it, and wearing their clothes. They had no idea of the disease and its dreadful nature.

"From the Chipaways it extended over all the Indians of the forest to it's northward extremity, and by the Sieux over the Indians of the Plains and crossed the Rocky Mountains. More men died in proportion than Women and Children, for unable to bear the heat of the fever, they rushed into the Rivers and Lakes to cool themselves, and the greater part thus perished. . . .

"All the Wolves and Dogs that fed on the bodies of those that died of the Small Pox lost their hair especially on the sides and belly and even for six years after many Wolves were found in this condition and their furs useless. The Dogs were mostly killed. . . .

"I have already mentioned that before that dreadful disease appeared among the Indians they were numerous, and the Bison, Moose, Red, and other Deer more so in proportion and Provisions of Meat, both fresh and dried in abundance. Of this all the Traders and Indians were fully sensible, and it was noted by the Traders and Natives that at the death of the latter, and their being thus reduced to a small number, the numerous herds of Bison and Deer also disappeared both in the Woods and in the Plains, and the Indians about Cumberland House declared the same of the Moose, and the Swans, Geese, and Ducks with the Gulls no longer frequented the Lakes in the same number they used to do; and where they had an abundance of eggs during the early part of the Summer, they had now to search to find them."

How swiftly smallpox, measles, and the lowly mumps decimated primitive people who had no immunity against them. But the amazing thing was to realize that other forms of life were affected as well. After a hundred and seventy-five years, the Indians had returned and the bones of the dead—if there were any left on the point—were covered deep with moss and duff.

Eric closed his book, and we dozed on the rocks.

"Bourgeois," said Omond, "your canoe was almost out of sight several times, and when the bow came up I never knew if you would make it over the top or not."

Denis gripped my arm. "This will pass, he means well."

We maneuvered the rest of the lake without difficulty, taking advantage of the wind whenever we could. The big open sweeps were over, but we could still feel the broken force of the wind between the islands. That afternoon we portaged Great Devil and Little Devil Rapids, doing some shooting, wading and lining down parts of the latter. Such awe-inspiring names as Rapids de Diable did not frighten us any more; we took them in our stride.

That night we camped on a rocky island before Otter Portage. There was a sunset and a new moon. This was our last camp before reaching the Hudson's Bay Post at Stanley. Almost half of the trip was behind us, some 230 miles, and supplies were running low. Now we could stock up, have such luxuries as bread and eggs. We would meet the clerk of the post and the Indians, would get news of the outside world and our mail. These things were in our minds that night. We were looking forward to them, but we also feared that something might happen to break up the party and change our plans. Our life so far had been simple and complete. We had settled down to a certain routine and outside of the vagaries of weather and terrain, there had been nothing to worry about except achieving our daily objective, making camp, and preparing food. It had been good to settle down.

Until that night, Stanley had been just another spot on the map, a spot circled in red, one of the major milestones of the expedition. Now it was close and we would see it before noon. Coming out of the bush is always an adventure, even though it is only to arrive at a trading post far removed from civilization. But all we wanted was to transact our business, pick up our supplies, and get under way again as swiftly as possible.

Omond sensed how we all felt and said: "There's the possibility of a camp site a few hours beyond Stanley. We can make it if we don't waste too much time. The map shows some small islands just this side of the rapids."

Before going to sleep, I heard the drone of an outboard motor to the south at Stanley Post. We would take Omond's advice and make the islands beyond.

CHAPTER 13

STANLEY POST

Embarked *about an hour be-fore daybreak—passed Rapid River discharge, Lac de la Montagne, Portage Montagne, Petit Roche, Otter Lake, Otter Portage, Portge. de Diable, and encamped here at seven P.M. with the Spoon and Coal's band of Indians consisting of twelve families; two of Mr. Clarke's men are along with them and they appear well disposed but have most extravagant notions; it is intended to equip these Indians without bringing them to Isle à la Crosse in order that they have no communication with the Nor. West, but*

*it was very injudicious to permit them to encamp on the track as,
if Thompson who is a great favorite falls in with them, it is
probable that he may debauch at least half of the band. Mr.
Clarke gave them a large Keg and they are now in a beastly state.*
—GEORGE SIMPSON (*1820*)

THE HUDSON'S BAY COMPANY means a great deal in the Canadian North. The sign with the date 1670 across the front of every post has meaning far beyond the matter of trade. The fact that the company has been operating for almost three hundred years without a break has given the organization an aura of dignity and permanence.

Everything revolves around the posts scattered from Labrador to Yukon and beyond. Missions are located there, and establishments of the Provincial and Dominion governments. The settlements themselves are usually named for the posts, as they are the core of all activity, of the social, economic, and spiritual life of the vast regions they service. There was the North West Company and others in the past, but during the last one hundred years all have disappeared except the Honourable Company of Adventurers.

As we neared the post at Stanley, we began to see many Indian fishing camps and motor-driven canoes. Although Stanley was only an outpost of civilization, for the moment the true wilderness seemed behind us. The closer we drew the more we were conscious of a subtle change not only in the feeling of the country but within ourselves. Something always happens to a crew at this point in any expedition. Somehow the old sense of freedom and completeness is dissipated, and men begin to think of things that have nothing to do with traveling through the bush. Until then, we had been dependent on one another not only in the matter of routine responsibilities but because of what each individual had come to mean. What we had done together had welded us into a unit.

I looked at my companions as we worked our way down Otter Lake: Eric with his meticulous arrangement of equipment, his painstaking planning and research into every minor detail long before the trip began, the way he sat in the bow or stern and how his nose peeled at the first touch of sun and wind; Denis with his black beard and navy sweater, how those massive shoulders could pull a paddle when bucking the waves, and how merry his laugh and French patois at the end of a day; Omond studying his maps and charts, his calmness, except when mixing a drink and discovering I had used up all the pots; Elliot with his zest for living and joy on the trail, his speed and concentration when helping me around the fire, the torn shorts he wore after tearing the bottom of his trousers to shreds on a brushy portage; Tony singing into the wind, "The Last Time I Saw Paris," his engrossment with fishing whenever we stopped, our pipes together every hour, and the moments before breakfast when he would join me for a cup of coffee in the half-light of dawn. A message at Stanley requiring someone to leave could change all this. The expedition would go on, but it would not be the same.

We carried Stony Mountain and Mountain portages and paddled down Mountain Lake, one of the most beautiful we had seen. It had high rocky shores and islands well-grown with old spruce, whose pointed tops were serrated evenly against the sky line. Evidently few fires had hit the area, or those that had occurred were close enough to Stanley to be put out in short order. There was little poplar or birch, only straight stands of unbroken spruce wherever we looked.

More and more Indian camps were now in evidence. Almost every island or point had some sort of shelter, with the inevitable fish nets hung to dry beside the smoking racks. We landed at one spot—a gray little tent in a clearing between the spruces. There was a smoldering fire under the rack, which was loaded with split whitefish turning golden brown. Someone must be tending the fire, but we could not see anyone. We walked up a rise to one side of the tent and found two little girls and a mangy dog. The parents, evidently out fishing, had left the pair to watch camp and the fire while they were gone. The girls were shy. They said nothing, but rewarded us with broad smiles when we gave them each a square of hard chocolate.

On the way to the canoe we stole a look into the tent. A pile of damp and grubby blankets was lying against the back wall in filthy disorder. The family would crawl into them for the night and shove them back into the same foul tangle in the morning.

Such camps disturbed me, for it is so easy to keep clean where there is plenty of water and sun and wind and the wish to use them. Not all camps are this way, but many were. This happens to whites as well as to Indians, and some of the dirtiest specimens I have seen in a lifetime in the bush were whites who appeared to have lost all respectability. I have noticed, too, that as soon as people become careless in the matters of cleanliness and order, morale deteriorates. One look at a tent or a cabin and you know much about the owner's personality and character.

Just before we made the final point above the village, we passed Shooting Up Rock. In the old days before the advent of the Mission, hunting and fishing parties of the Indians used to stop there and, with a jack-pine bow, shoot an arrow toward the top of the cliff. If the arrow went over the top, it was considered a good omen. If it fell short, the party returned to the village. So many parties failed in their bid for good luck that often the people went hungry for long periods of time rather than tempt the fates.

The first missionary from England accompanied an expedition to the shooting place and with great courage broke the arrows and told the Indians to go on. Luckily there was no bloodshed. The party continued, and because the expedition was highly successful, the superstition died out.

We rounded a final point. There lay the village of Stanley, the red roofs of the Hudson's Bay Company buildings, the white church, the clustered cabins and shacks. Long before we arrived, huskies howled their welcome and a crowd of people gathered at the dock. Word of our coming had preceded us. As the canoes slid alongside, the Indians solemnly looked over our outfit and held the canoes fast as we disembarked.

Canon Rupert Taylor and his wife were also there to meet us, having flown in for the services on Sunday. They took us over to the big white church, of which they were very proud, and told us that about ninety Indians would be in attendance, in spite of the fact that many were away on fishing expeditions and had nets to tend. He showed us the heating stove in the center of the church. It was a primitive cast-iron affair with the longest cabin stovepipe I had ever seen running straight up through a hole in the roof. It must have been at least sixty feet from the stove to the hole where the pipe disappeared, exactly as it would have done in a cabin. It was a miracle, according to the Canon, that the pipe was kept repaired, since Indians hate to climb high places. Such a pipe actually required the services of a good steeplejack.

The Hudson's Bay Post was like all the others we had seen— a small store painted white, with a red roof and the conventional sign in front, *Hudson's Bay Company Incorporated 1670*. The building itself was about sixteen by twenty-four feet and resembled any little country store. It was stocked with the usual Indian trade goods and supplies, guns, ammunition and fishing tackle, leather dog harnesses, tump lines, calico in bolts, moccasins, rubbers, coarse cotton stockings, pants and shirts and dresses. In front of the store were three new square-stern canoes, priced from $300 to $350. Every Indian wanted one, but at that price it would take years to acquire, not to mention the motor.

As I wandered around this modern post looking at the assortment of manufactured goods, foodstuffs, cans, the innumerable items found in any backwoods store, I could not help but contrast the stocks of trade goods of the old days, not only of the established fur companies, but of the free traders and *coureurs de bois* who swarmed throughout the Northwest a hundred and fifty years ago. It had been different then, entirely different, for everything that came in was carried by canoe and on the backs of men. Now it was flown in or freighted by tractors and sleds during the winter. The beads were still there and the blankets and guns and iron works, but the guns were modern, the shells in shiny cardboard boxes, and there was no wine or rum.

A diary entry of Alexander Henry the Younger of the North West Company on July 2, 1800, at Grand Portage tells the story. It could have been duplicated for dozens of brigades leaving that post for the Athabasca and Churchill River trade.

"The canoes having been given out to the men, to gum and prepare, I found everything ready for our departure; and early this morning gave out to all their respective loading, which consisted of 28 packages per canoe, assorted for the Salteur trade on Red River, namely:

Merchandise, 90 pounds each	5 bales
Canal tobacco	1 bale
Kettles	1 bale
Guns	1 case
Iron works	1 case
New twist tobacco	2 rolls
Leaden balls	2 bags

Leaden shot	1 bag
Flour	1 bag
Sugar	1 keg
Gunpowder	2 kegs
High wine—9 gallons each	10 kegs

"Equipage for the voyage: Provisions for four men to Red River, 4 bags of corn, 1½ bushels in each, private property belonging to the men, consisting of clothing, tobacco, etc., for themselves and families for the year; so that when all hands embarked, the canoes sunk to the gunnel.

"At ten o'clock the brigades were all off and at three o'clock I followed. The water was very low. In a short time we came to Partridge portage, of about 600 paces over.

"The road was very slippery and muddy. Having got our baggage over, we embarked and proceeded to the Prairie where our people were camped. All were merry over their favorite regale, which is always given on their departure, and generally enjoyed at this spot, where we have a delightful meadow to pitch our tents and plenty of elbow room for the men's antics."

But furs went across the counter as they did in the old days, and Indians were given credit even as then. Families drew their supplies and settled up in the spring.

An Indian girl came in and bought a pair of brown cotton stockings, two cans of beans, and a can of marmalade.

A little boy bought some hard candy and a package of Eastman Kodak film.

A group of women watched us with interest as we made our purchases. They talked softly in Cree and smiled when we looked their way. At last we were through. The clerk asked if there was anything more he could do for us and invited us cordially to spend the night. We explained that we were behind schedule and must get down the lake as far as possible before dark. We asked about the country ahead, wrote a few letters, and sent out our films.

Courtesy and co-operation is a tradition with the Hudson's Bay Company, and Stanley Post was no exception. The supplies we had arranged for at Winnipeg were all packed and ready for us, and our messages and letters were all in one package. There was no disturbing news, no plans to change. We would continue as we had begun.

About four in the afternoon our boxes were carried down to the landing and the supplies transferred to the almost empty food packs. We loaded the canoes, waved good-by, and started down the river, paddling past the big white church, the scattered cabins, and the snarling dogs tethered at the shore who howled and strained as we slipped by. I was impressed by the size of the church, its huge whiteness way out there in the bush. On Sunday the beach in front of it would be lined with canoes. The Indians would come in their very best attire, for going to church has not only religious significance; it is a chance to visit, meet friends, and talk about things of importance in the Churchill River country.

On the way down the lake we passed a uranium claim where

the top of a granite knob had been blasted to expose the ore. The pink rock had a raw and ugly scar. We then remembered the Geiger counter that Omond and Denis had taken along and the prospecting permits which they had provided for themselves. So far we had just played at prospecting. Whenever we happened to stop on some rocky shelf or outcrop, we listened for the ticking that indicates promising ore. We had found that regular ticking occurs almost everywhere but that over veins of pink pegmatite it was louder and more agitated. When we saw that claim, we decided we had been far too lackadaisical in our efforts, that in the future we would investigate all outcrops of pink granite more industriously and perhaps locate a claim. After all, we were traversing country most of which had never been prospected seriously before and our Geiger counter was as good as anyone's.

But no one could generate the necessary enthusiasm. We were far too busy traveling down the route of the explorers to do any prospecting. Such matters seemed out of place on an expedition devoted to the intangible resources of wilderness. It would be like estimating the board feet in a preserve of virgin timber or trying to figure out the amount of pigment in an old masterpiece. Somehow it seemed incongruous to find a mine in country we had come to enjoy.

As Omond said: "What on earth would we do with a uranium mine if we did find one?"

Several miles down the lake and well out of sight of the village and the narrows we found a tiny spit of an island in the center of the channel. It was barely large enough to take care of the tents and the fire, with space left for the canoes. It was as compact a little setup as we had ever known.

A sunset was coming up and occasionally even at that distance we could hear the long howls of the huskies. Contact had been made with the outside, nothing had happened to disrupt our plans, and once more we were on our way. We had covered 260 miles and were over halfway to our goal. It was good to be on our own again and to know we would be together to the end.

That night for variety we had food out of cans—meatballs and spaghetti. When I saw those tins on the shelf in the store, I could not resist buying them. Perhaps it was the picture on the outside, a tempting picture of someone else's cooking. It would be a welcome change from fish, stew, or bacon, but it didn't taste nearly as good as we had anticipated. We also had fresh store bread instead of bannock, and even that seemed flat and without substance. The voyageurs were becoming bush rats and liking bush fare.

After supper that night Eric told us the story of the naming of the Rapids of the Drowned on the Slave River to the west:

"According to the diary of one of the traders, a party of two canoes including women and children approached the rapids. None of them were familiar with the river, but the one experienced canoeman in the group decided to go ahead with three of the young men to see if the water was safe enough to run. Before going down, he told the men in the waiting canoe he would fire a single shot as a signal to proceed, if all went well.

"The rapids turned out to be very dangerous and difficult, but after a hair-raising run they finally made the bank below. Just as they were preparing to walk back upstream to help the others portage, one of the young men, not knowing of the signal agreed upon and to the dismay of the guide, fired a single shot at a flock of ducks. The shot could not be recalled, and the second canoe bore down the river and all in it were drowned."

"Let that be a lesson to all of us," said Denis, "no silent agreements."

Eric then read an excerpt from Mackenzie's diary: "The direct navigation continued to be through rivers and canals interrupted by rapids; and the distance to the first Decharge is four miles in a westerly direction. Then follows Lac de la Montaigne which runs south-southwest three miles and a half, then north six miles through narrow channels formed by islands and continues northwest five miles to the lake of the same name which is no sooner crossed than another appears in sight leading to Otter Lake from where it is nine miles westerly to Otter Portage."

Prosaic notes in a traveler's diary. Exactly the sort of thing Denis was jotting down each night of our trip. Such simple entries were of vital importance to any expedition which might follow. To realize others a century and a half ago had made such notations on terrain that had changed very little gave us a sense of oneness with the past and a feeling of companionship with all those who had gone before.

What we were doing, however, was nothing compared to what they had done with poor maps or none at all, unreliable guides, little food except what they killed, no protection from insects or the weather. In addition to the physical hazards of unknown country, there was always the threat of being ambushed on portages or being attacked at night. What small hardships we encountered were trivial by comparison. Our only problem was to make our rendezvous on time and to make it safely.

CHAPTER 14

NISTOWIAK

W̶ERE *afloat this morning at day-break, and found Mr. Clarke at the Grande Rapid, where one of his men impertinently told me that unless the gallon of rum was paid, his Master authorized them to turn the bag of shot out of the canoe, I therefore ordered my people to bring it on, until they overtook the brigade, altho' the canoe is loaded to the water's edge; proceeded 'till nine O'Clock when we breakfasted and dried our baggage, which has been wet several days. Made Portage de Baril, Portage de Isle, and Rapid River Portage, at the entrance of Rapid River* [Montreal] *found some of Mr. Clarke's people belonging to the Lac la Ronge Post waiting his arrival; he is likely to be warmly opposed there this season and altho' his first Brigade has been in nearly a month, there is not a piece of goods yet sent to the Post. This is very bad management. Stopped here the remainder of the day.*

—GEORGE SIMPSON (*1820*)

OMOND AND I had agreed at the beginning of the trip that at the halfway mark we would change bowmen, so Tony shifted to my canoe and Denis to his. Elliot and Eric, who changed positions every day, continued as they were.

"Farewell, Bourgeois," said Denis as he and Omond paddled off. "Eet ees a sad parting, *n'est-ce pas?*"

As we portaged Stanley Rapids and entered Drop Lake we could see a smudge of smoke, some buildings, and another uranium mine far to the southwest. The sun glittered on the shiny new roofs, and I could not help but think again of what Hemingway said about Africa, "A continent ages quickly once we come."

That smudge of smoke was a sign of progress, but now those ridges of ice-polished granite were no longer young. In the space of a year they had been plunged into the nuclear age.

Eric informed us that he had had a most cordial letter from Marcel Pouchon, one of the owners of the uranium mine, inviting us to visit on our way through. While we appreciated this very much, we decided to push toward Nistowiak Falls. There were many miles to go before nightfall.

We landed where the river entered the lake and found the old portage, or rather what was left of it, for a great ragged gouge ran from the water's edge. A bulldozer had made a road, and the boulders were pushed to one side and the trees piled in confusion. The roadway was about twelve feet wide, with the marks of the huge machine still plain. Only in a few places, where it curved around a rock or a big tree, had the portage survived. Like any other portage in the country, it was about a foot wide and two or three inches deep in the duff. There were only about twenty feet of it undisturbed, all that was left of a trail over which Indians and voyageurs had carried their bark canoes and ninety-pound *pièces* since the trade began. Here was the gateway to Lac la Ronge and the river known as Montreal, here where it joined the Churchill was a major route to Saskatchewan and to York Factory on Hudson Bay.

According to George Simpson, Lac la Ronge had had an establishment for trade since the year 1782. An important outpost of the Hudson's Bay Company, the Rapid River—now known as the Montreal—had been a highway to the north and east. Administered from Ile à la Crosse, like most interior establishments it had had its ups and downs, was burned repeatedly and rebuilt, and was finally abandoned about 1830 because the country surrounding it was exhausted of game and fur.

That little section of trail had seen many things—on spring days when flood waters almost covered it and the spruces were full of siskins, redpolls, and whitethroats coming through; in the summer when fur brigades labored up its winding course;

in the fall when aspen leaves covered it with gold; and in winter when drifts lay deep and a snowshoe trail followed it from the smooth unbroken highway of the lake. For hundreds of years there had been no change, and now the old portage was gone and a new era had been ushered in.

We left what remained of the old trail and trudged up the muddy tractor road toward the top. Even though things had changed, there was still the old thrill of portaging around a falls, the increasing roar until the whole canyon becomes filled with it and the air is vibrant and electric with the power of plunging water, the growing mist and lushness and color and a sense of vitality in all growing things. When I carry a load up such a trail, there is no great consciousness of weight or weariness.

Within fifty feet of the summit, a path branched off to the left. Now close to the source of the great sound, we hurried forward to where the river plunged over its precipice. We stopped on a little shelf to one side of the brink. There before us was a green wall of water so clear the rocks showed plainly underneath, a wall slipping smoothly to the river below. All around us now was the thunder, and below was a confusion of white and green. How long we stood there I do not know for in such places time is forgotten. Forgotten too was the bull-dozed road and the mine and the blasted granite hillside. We were back in the days when the north was young and unchanged.

I turned to get a better view and there to my surprise was a neat little sign in black and white, Nistowiak Falls. I looked at it in dismay, not that there was anything wrong with the sign or with such a fine public gesture by the officials of the uranium mine; what startled me was that it was there at all in the Lonely Land. Somehow it seemed out of place in a country where the names of Mackenzie, Primeau, Frobisher, and David Thompson were still fresh. Even more than the scar of the road or the mine itself, that little sign pointed the path of things to come and made me realize that the days of the old wilderness along the Churchill were numbered, that in my time and not too many years hence, there would be a great change.

We sat above the falls, a drop of perhaps forty or fifty feet, and studied the smooth brown ledge over which the water plunged, the emerald of ferns and mosses on the rocks of the gorge. After a time we worked our way back down the road to the canoes, got in and pushed ahead to a rocky point beside a rapids where the mine had built a fishing camp. The rapids were beautiful, and we ate our lunch beside them.

While we sat there, two Indians appeared with a big husky dog.

"Good fishing here," said one of them pointing to a screened-in cleaning table covered with scales. "Mine bosses catch many big ones."

They explained they were going hunting down the river and would guide us through the rapids if we wished. We accepted gladly, never having known the luxury of a guided tour down fast water.

The rapids were mild compared to many we had run, and

we drifted along easily behind the Indians, round bend after bend, riffle after riffle, avoiding spouts and swirls exactly as they did until we were safe in the quiet waters below. Our guides turned then and waved us on. They pulled their canoe up on the bank and struck off with their rifles into the woods. A little later we heard two sharp reports from the direction in which they had gone.

We had seen little game since our start, which was not surprising down such a major route of travel as the Churchill. For two centuries, voyageurs' brigades had traveled the great river, killing any game they saw to augment their meager rations. Indians had done the same, and even today it was seldom that any group traveled without keeping a sharp eye out for anything in the way of food. No moose or deer or caribou had much of a chance if it frequented the area. Only up the tributary streams, in the lakes and ponds off the major route was there game to be seen. The boys had no doubt spotted something on one of their exploring trips into the interior and knew exactly where they were going, for not more than twenty minutes had elapsed since they left us on the river.

We passed through Drinking Lake, a name that conjured up visions of indiscretions of voyageurs in the care of a vital part of their cargo. Or it might have been the Indians themselves, for the use of rum in the trade was an accepted practice and the debauchery involved was evident in every trader's diary. Alexander Henry the Younger noted in 1801:

"Indians having asked for liquor and having promised to decamp and hunt well all summer, I gave them some. Grande

Guerde stabbed Capot Rouge, Le Boef stabbed his young wife in the arm. . . . Little Shell almost beat his mother's brains out with a club. . . . I sowed garden seeds."

Everywhere the traders went the precious kegs of rum went with them. The men of the North West Company were the worst offenders, for they seemed to have the greatest supply, far greater, according to the records, than that of the Hudson's Bay Company. The results were always the same: the continued degeneration of native tribes and their growing dependence on firewater. No wonder there were names such as Keg and Drinking Lake.

We were back on the trail again with all its feeling of the past. Nistowiak, the bulldozed portage, the little sign, the new fishing camp at the rapids with its screened-in fish-cleaning table—all that now seemed unreal. It was as if we had passed through an unpleasantness on the route, like a recent burn with blackened trees, or a blowdown with spruces lying like jackstraws, and now were in good country again.

That afternoon we spied an island with a broad sloping shelf of rock facing the west in the full blaze of the sun. We stopped paddling, got out the glasses and looked it over. No one said a word but all had the same idea. Though it was only three o'clock and we had come only part of the way we had planned, the temptation to make an early camp, wash our clothes, and spread the damp outfit out to dry again was too inviting to resist. Not since Black Bear Island Lake had we had such a chance, and not since Dipper when Eric was sick had we enjoyed any serious loafing. It would be good to shave, swim leisurely, and possibly just sit for a few hours with nothing to do at all.

Omond turned to me. "Well?" he said.

I dipped my paddle and headed toward the island, and in a moment all three canoes were racing. We made it in record time and within minutes that shelf a hundred feet long by twenty wide was strewn with an amazing collection of shirts, socks, trousers and miscellaneous wearing apparel, for everything we owned had become soiled and wet from repeated drenchings by rain and spray. The down sleeping bags, which had begun to smell of mold, were draped over bushes and trees where the sun could work its magic. Tents were pitched with the sides unstaked so they could blow in the wind. Ponchos, air mattresses, even the cooking outfit, were laid out to dry, along with every item of food that had come this far with us since Ile à la Crosse.

No one can really appreciate ease without work, or the luxury of warmth and dryness unless they have suffered cold and wet under the spur of constant travel. On Dipper the outfit had been still dry and well-packed, our clothes clean. While it was good to stay there for a day we had not really deserved the break, but now we did, and as we walked around on the smooth shelf of rock we were in a gay and happy mood.

Tony, by way of celebration, cut off enough boughs for both tents from a down spruce he found. He called when he was through and invited me to lie down on the bed he had prepared just for a taste of what the night held in store.

Omond, Elliot, and Denis had pitched their tent about fifty

feet down from ours and had a front yard all to themselves. Eric as usual had placed his one-man tent in utter seclusion, beyond the rock itself. Denis and I built a fireplace near the water on a perfectly flat section of rock which served both as kitchen and drying place. Within an hour we had developed the most luxurious camp site we had known on the trip.

"Isn't it queer," remarked Denis, looking up from his diary, "here we work like beavers getting everything set as if we were planning to stay a month. Then in the morning we tear everything down, throw it all in the packs, and without another look take off for someplace else." He shook his head sadly. "Bourgeois, it just doesn't make sense."

It was true; we would leave it all behind in a matter of hours. But there was great satisfaction in doing things that had been postponed or impossible during ordinary traveling days. Just spending a little more time getting a tent perfectly pitched or putting some extra touches to the fireplace were distinct pleasures. Certainly we would leave without compunction in the morning, but that did not mean we had not enjoyed to the fullest every extra preparation.

That night after a swim, with everything under cover, we sat around in the level rays of the setting sun and watched an eagle soar. When it turned into the sun its silver head shone in the light. It was watching us. Higher and higher it went, and once we heard it scream. The bird turned with a final flash of silver, then disappeared beyond the ridge.

This was our twelfth camp. We had covered about 275 miles. In the morning we would go through Trade Lake and there meet Elliot's old friend Harry Moody, the prospector and archaeologist who was making a study of ancient Indian camp sites and the first trading posts in the region.

"I found an old mine detector," said Elliot, "and shipped it up to him. He's been finding all kinds of things with it ever since."

"Strange procedure for a general of the Canadian army," said Omond. "How can you justify such a diversion of valuable government property?"

Elliot laughed. "He'll probably have sufficient stuff to start a museum. That will be justification enough, and in the public interest as well."

A wan quarter-moon hung high, hung there as a reminder of the glory to come when it was full. From a vantage point such as ours, it would be a sight worth waiting for. I could imagine it hanging over the horizon pulsating and heavy. It would struggle free from the entangling spruce tops, pale, climb high, and the wilderness would be bathed in its light. How the loons would call on such a night! All down the waterway, at every village and encampment, the dogs would strain at their leashes and sing the whole night through. A loon did call and was answered far down the lake. Then the dusk closed in.

This was the Lonely Land, a big country that could absorb a hundred uranium mines, many more Hudson's Bay Posts and airplane fishing camps, and there would still be places no one would ever see. The Canadian North is big enough, I reasoned, to take it all with room to spare, for there will always be vast areas of no economic importance along the smaller watersheds and off the beaten track. But even as I reassured myself, I wondered if it was actually true, if in this day of man's ability to reshape the face of the earth, even this great rocky land would be big enough to withstand his onslaughts.

The explorers had passed this little island—the Frobishers in 1775 on their way to Ile à la Crosse, Peter Pond on his way to the thirteen-mile portage known as Methye when he was going to Athabasca in 1778, and Alexander Mackenzie in 1785. They too were using the riches of the north, but in their use they left few marks and did not change the ancient terrain. They saw the same skylines, the same old burns, the same glacial markings on the rocks. They had come over the famous portage we would see in the morning, Portage de Traite.

By the time we were through with supper there was an increase of light in the north. Long before the northern lights would blaze, however, we would be in our bags and sound asleep.

Eric came over and stood beside me and we watched the sky.

"Peter Pond," he said, "could not remember having met anyone who had ever heard the northern lights make any noise, but on still nights he had definitely heard them make a rustling and crackling noise 'like the waving of a large flag in a fresh gale of wind.' "

"I've still to hear it," I said, "but if Pond says so there must be something to it."

"If they crackle toward midnight, wake me."

We both laughed, knowing full well that on such a night there wasn't a chance. The dishes were washed and stacked carefully beside the food packs, everything was covered with the big tarp, and the canoes and paddles were safe. All was snug for the night.

Before I went into the tent, I walked down to the shore for a final look. The lights were beginning to play. Pond, I knew, had written his description during the winter when the heavens could really flame. This was only August, with nights seldom dark enough for a display. "Like the waving of a large flag in a fresh gale of wind." Perhaps some night if I listened carefully, I'd hear them whisper and crackle too.

CHAPTER 15

FROG SKIN PORTAGE

HAVING *passed them, it is nec-
essary to cross Portage de Traite, or as it is called by the Indians
Athiquisipichigan Ouinigam, or the Portage of the Stretched
Frog-Skin, to the Missinipi. The waters already described discharge themselves into Lake Winipic, and augment those of the
river Nelson. These which we are now entering are called the
Missinipi, or great Churchill River.*

*All the country to the south and east of this, within the line of
progress that has been described, is intersperced by lakes, hills,
and rivers, and is full of animals of the fur kind, as well as the*

191

moose-deer. Its inhabitants are the Knisteneaux Indians, who are called by the servants of the Hudson's Bay Company, at York, their home guards.

—Alexander Mackenzie

WE LEFT OUR CAMP SITE on Drinking Lake at six thirty in the morning, feeling that we must get under way while the wind was down to make up for the afternoon of the day before. When the canoes were loaded I strolled around the ledge for a final look. The fireplace was cold and gray; the tent sites with their flattened beds of spruce and stacked poles were already impersonal. We were leaving as unceremoniously as if they had never belonged to us. A few pictures would remind us, but even they would have a certain unreality about them. What we would remember best was the feeling of quiet and leisure we had known for a few hours after many days of activity.

At the end of the lake we turned left into a fast narrows, shot the first rapids without difficulty and portaged the second into Keg Lake. It had begun to rain, and the sky was growing darker. Heavy black clouds were in the distance. We began to see more birds: ducks rising on all sides, a swarm of terns screaming constantly above us, and in the distance great flocks of pelicans snow-white against the sky. We were glad to see them for it meant that this particular area was untraveled and undisturbed. We could see them floating like patches of foam far ahead of the canoes. As we drew close they would lift into the wind and soar over us wing tip to wing tip just as we had seen them that first day on Ile à la Crosse.

Here we saw four grayish birds alighting like puffs of down on the water. Each had a single dusky spot on top of the head and back of the eye. These were the first Bonaparte's gulls we had encountered. We sped after them just for the joy of seeing them drift off the surface and then, without any apparent sense of weight, settle down again. Never had we seen such a gravity-defying demonstration of flight. This was swamp country and not since the Haultain marshes were there so many birds. Even Mackenzie spoke of them:

"The numerous flocks of wildfowl that frequent it in the spring and fall make a most desirable spot for the constant residence of some and the occasional rendezvous of others of the inhabitants of the country, particularly the Knisteneaux."

The birds above were the same species that circled the birchbark canoes of the old brigades. The voyageurs had heard the same screaming of the terns, had watched the flight of countless mallards up and down the river, had no doubt marveled as we did at the aliveness in the area.

For eight miles we paddled in rain and mist, portaged around Keg Falls at the lower end, and three miles below that made the Grand Rapids portage into Trade Lake. The rain increased, and black clouds hung low. I watched the sky, remembering other days, with the uneasy feeling we should not continue. Already wet and wanting to make the end of the lake for our meeting with Harry Moody, we decided to push on. We would take a chance and head for shore only if travel became impossible.

Two hours later we were approaching the end of the lake. An island lay ahead with what looked like a high rocky shore —the only possibility of a camp site we had seen. The sky was very dark now, and though we knew a thorough drenching was in the offing, we covered the packs with ponchos and decided to make a dash for it. There was little wind; an ominous hush told us of what was to come. The cloud mass above grew more and more threatening, and over the horizon was a flash of lightning. The first half-mile went well. During the second, it began to rain steadily—the sort of downpour that soaks everything and shows no sign of letting up. Water was creeping up to the bottoms of the packs, even though they were raised by sticks laid over the ribs. We were now within a quarter mile of the island, and the clouds emptied all they held. In a matter of minutes the packs were standing in water. We paddled desperately, reached the shore, hauled out the canoes, emptied them, covered the packs with a tarpaulin, and took what shelter we could under the trees. The place was far too rough for a camp site; I knew we would have to move on as soon as the rain let up.

An hour later, with the storm over, we loaded the canoes once more and paddled on toward the end of the lake. An Indian family was camped in a little bay to the south, and just beyond we stopped at another encampment of several families, possibly twenty people. They told us they were fishing for one of the filleting plants of Lac la Ronge, that a plane came in twice a week to take their catch. Most of the men were young. They lined up on the slippery dock of spruce poles they had built and looked us over with a certain disdain, wondering, I am sure, what important business made it necessary for us to travel in the rain.

We also looked them over with some curiosity. Why for instance, should they pick such a swampy place for a camp, a place without sun or wind, a hidden bay soggy and damp in the rain and swarming with flies and mosquitoes on a warm day in June? Seldom do they ever pick a spot for its beauty or any particular convenience except protection from cold and wind. Only white men seem to care about a view. Perhaps, I thought, we would not be so concerned either if we had not deprived ourselves of scenery in the lives we lead and were not starved for vistas and horizons. With Indians, basic utilities are always the deciding factors in picking a camping place: wood, water, and shelter. Nothing else is important.

As we got ready to leave, one of the men said: "Harry Moody waiting at Frog Portage."

We left the fishing camp and proceeded down the lake, found a camp site at the east end of a long rocky spit of an island about a mile from the portage into the Sturgeon Weir. Miraculously, the sun had come out and we hastily hung the tents and all our drenched equipment to dry. There was plenty of wood, and in spite of the flood we soon had a fire going. While we were waiting for supper, Eric read about Frog Skin Portage from the diary.

"The Portage de Traite," said Mackenzie, "as has already been hinted, received its name from Mr. Joseph Frobisher who penetrated into this part of the country from Canada as early as the years 1774 and 1775 where he met with the Indians in the spring, on their way to Churchill, according to annual custom, with their canoes full of valuable furs. They traded with him for as many of them as his canoes could carry, and in consequence of this transaction, the Portage received and has since retained its present appellation. He also denominated these waters The English River. The Missinipi is the name it received from the Knisteneaux, when they first came to this country, and either destroyed or drove back the natives, whom they held in great contempt, on many accounts, but particularly for their ignorance in hunting the beaver, as well as in preparing, stretching, and drying the skins of these animals. And as a sign of their derision, they stretched the skin of a frog, and hung it up at the Portage. This was, at that time the utmost extent of their conquest or wayfaring progress west!!!! The river here which bears the appearance of a lake, takes its name from the Portage and is full of islands. Then succeed falls and cascades which form what is called the Grand Rapid."

While we were eating supper, a motor-driven canoe came out of the portage bay and headed toward us. We watched with interest as it bore down directly on our point. A white man sat regally in the center, and an Indian woman perched high in the bow. A man in the stern was running the motor.

"Harry Moody!" shouted Elliot, running down to the shore. "As I'm alive, the old prospector himself."

Willing hands grasped the gunwales as the canoe drifted in. The woman jumped lightly onto the rocks with the tow rope and tied it around a birch. Elliot introduced us to Harry and he in turn to Angélique and her husband, William Merasty.

"The moccasin telegraph," reported Moody, "informed us an hour ago that the white men had landed, turned over their canoes and started a fire."

We invited them all to have supper with us but they refused saying they had already had tea and rice.

"Been looking for some of the ancient Chippewyan fire-places," said Moody, "those rounded mounds of stone that marked their stopping places. Then, too, I've been on the trail of Louis Primeau who was in here trading with the Frobishers before the days of Alexander Mackenzie. In fact I think I've found the site of his house on a little point to one side of Frog Skin Portage. Wait until you see what I've dug up with my mine detector."

Harry Moody was gaunt and powerful. He had been in the bush prospecting and trading most of his life, but I could see that his real love was the past. When he talked about his explorations his eyes lighted and his animation belied his years. Here was the true archaeologist who was not only indefatigable in his search but because of his love for the country could interpret the past far better than someone whose interest was based solely on artifacts. After a disability suffered in the First

World War, followed by the death of his wife, he had headed for the wilds with the dream of piecing together the history of the Churchill River country.

Angélique, the Indian woman, did not join the men, but sat by herself close to the fireplace and the bow of the canoe. As a Cree, she knew her place and did not interfere or make herself busy as long as the men were around. Far better-looking than the average, with fine teeth and a good smile, she was dressed neatly, wore a good wool jacket in blue and black, and dark woolen trousers with beaded moccasins tied neatly around her ankles. When I walked to the fireplace to get the teapot, I lit a cigarette and, as an afterthought, handed one to her. She took it without a word and, when I handed her a flaming splinter, lit up without a sign of recognition. I left her puffing away contentedly and went back to the group. When I returned a second time, I gave her a cup of tea. This was also accepted without a word or change of expression, but I sensed that she was pleased.

Harry Moody, seeing what I had done, told us that Angélique was not only an excellent cook but one of the best birchmark chewers in the north, that she could make strange and beautiful designs with her teeth and might show us how if she were sure we were friendly and interested.

"This bark chewing," he explained, "is an ancient skill lost to most Indians today. Some Cree women can still do it, and Angélique is one of the best."

It was then he told us the story of Eskimo Charley who had lived in the area. He had a moose to plow his clearing near the portage. As the crowning event of his career, he had taken his family by canoe down the Mississippi to the Gulf of Mexico, then up the Atlantic coast and back to Montreal by way of the St. Lawrence, getting help from every community en route as well as the signatures of the mayor of every town through which he passed. According to Moody, he had finally retired to the barren grounds and died alone, surrounded by Eskimo skulls. He was one of the fabulous characters of the north, and his expedition rivaled those of the explorers who had preceded him.

After a couple of hours of visiting, Moody, Angélique, and William Merasty roared back the way they had come. They had invited us to stop by in the morning.

The big canoe slipped out of sight into the bay, and the motor was heard no more. That was where we would go, over the portage from the Churchill River to the headwaters of the Sturgeon Weir. It was our last night on the big river; the Weir would carry us to Flin Flon and possibly Cumberland House.

"Can you beat it," said Elliot, "he's really found a lot of stuff with that old mine detector, probably covered every foot of ground around the portage by now."

"That birchbark business interests me," said Omond. "It would be nice if we could get Angélique to do some for us."

"I've got plans," I said. "The tea and rice they had for supper sounds as though they might be short of food. I'll see what we can spare and persuade them to accept a gift."

From our camp site we could see where the Churchill

veered northeast to meet the Reindeer River, the route to the Fond du Lac country and Athabasca. For almost fifty miles this tributary extends due north, flowing from Reindeer Lake, a huge body of water almost a hundred and fifty miles in length. I knew this was the way David Thompson went and the way we, too, might go another year. It was a crossroads of travel; no wonder trading posts were established here.

By the time we had cleaned up the supper dishes and had everything stowed away it was almost ten o'clock, far later than we usually went to bed. The stars were bright, and well they might be, after the washing the air had received. The dripping from the trees had stopped. It would be a good day for our start down the Sturgeon Weir.

CHAPTER 16

PELICAN NARROWS

THE *Lake de Bouleau then fol-
lows. This lake might with greater propriety be denominated
a canal as it is no more than a mile in breadth. Its course is
rather to the east of north for twelve miles to Portage de L'Isle.
From thence there is still water to Portage de'Epinettes, except
an adjoining rapid. The distance is not more than four miles
westerly. After crossing this Portage it is not more than two
miles to Lake Miron which is in latitude 55.7 North. Its length*

*is about twelve miles and its breadth irregular, from two to
ten miles. It is only separated from Lake du Chitique or Pelican
Lake by a short, narrow, and small strait. That lake is not more
than seven miles long, and its course about north-west. The
Lake des Bois then succeeds, the passage to which is through
small lakes, separated by falls and rapids.*

—Alexander Mackenzie

THE NEXT MORNING, after waiting until the tents and outfits
were dry, we packed and headed for Frog Portage. As soon
as we entered the bay we could see the white tent with a big
fly and the canoe drawn up on the beach. Moody was waiting
for us, but to our disappointment William and Angélique were
not around.

"William is sick," he explained, "and Angélique is tending
him in the tent."

He must have seen my concern and the little bundle of food
in my hand, for he smiled and said: "For Angélique?"

I nodded and explained it was some extra food I had saved
out, figuring they might be running short.

"Put it on the rock," he said, so I placed the bag with the
beans, raisins, dried fruit and bacon where she could see it
when she came out. "She'll like that," he added. "It might
mean some good birchbark designs."

He showed us the little pool where Angélique had speared
a dozen jack fish the day before and how she cooked them by

splitting them open and lacing them over a birch frame for broiling. He showed us another way in which a sharp stick is forced down the gullet of a fish, the end of it stuck in the ground near the fire and turned until it is done.

"After being cooked," explained Moody, "the skin and scales peel off easily and there is all the white meat, tender and clean, no fuss or bother at all. It's the easiest way to prepare a fish in the bush, and for Indians it is perfect. Twelve Indians sitting around a fire, 12 jack fish, 12 sticks, all very simple. And besides, it gives each one something to do."

We gathered on a smooth flat rock just off the portage and actually in the bed of a little spillover flowing from the Churchill. The creek was low. In the spring the rock was under water, as the polishing showed. The place marked an overflow point. Should its bed be eroded a few feet, it could rob the great river of much of its water, a feat of river piracy not uncommon in the drainages of the continent.

Here Harry Moody laid out his precious artifacts: bits of Indian pottery, willowware, shilling flour tokens once used as currency in the trade, clay-pipe bowls and stems, flintrocks from old guns, beaver hooks and spears and many other treasures. A beaver hook intrigued me particularly. The shaft was about two feet long, the hook itself a murderous thing with a vicious barb. Samuel Hearne described its use:

"Persons attempting to take beaver in winter should be well acquainted with their manner of life. They have many holes in the nearby banks which serve as places of retreat when an injury is offered to their houses. In general it is in these holes that they are taken by the Indians. On a small river or creek, the Indians some-times find it necessary to stake a river across, to prevent the animals from escaping. Afterwards they endeavor to find out all the holes or places of retreat under the banks. Each man, being furnished with an ice-chisel, lashes it to a staff four or five feet long. He then walks along the shore, knocking the chisel against the ice. Those who are well acquainted with the work can tell by the sound of the ice when they have found a beaver hole or vault. They then cut a hole through the ice big enough to admit an old beaver.

"While they are about this work, some of the women and under-strappers are busy breaking open the house. At times this is no easy task for I have known these houses to be five or six feet thick, and one I saw was eight feet thick at the crown. But when the beavers find that their house is being invaded, they flee to the holes in the banks for shelter.

"Perceiving their movements by the agitation of the water at the holes, the waiting Indians immediately block up the entrances to the vaults with stakes. They then haul the beaver out, either by hand or with a large hook fastened to the end of a stick."

I turned the hook over and over. It was still very sharp, could catch in a beaver's soft hide as efficiently as ever. I could not help but think of the cruelty and suffering that had gone into the great fortunes based on the fur trade, considerations always taken for granted and dismissed as unimportant sentimentalism. Fur was for human use and to be harvested.

From now on we would see more beaver signs, but coming

down the Churchill we had seldom seen the peeled aspen or birch sticks that indicated their feeding. For possibly a hundred years there had been few beaver along such intensely traveled highways as the Churchill. Beaver were still currency as they were then and few houses were unmolested if they were within easy reach.

We walked across the creek and finally came to a little point where Moody had used his mine detector.

"Here," he said, "was the site of Louis Primeau's cabin, built long before the explorers came through."

"You have no idea," he said to Elliot, "how wonderful it is to walk around with the detector telling me where to dig." For a hundred feet the earth was pitted with holes, each a foot or two deep, some just beneath the surface.

This was the trading post of the man who had given his name to the lake where we met Father Moraud, the man Simpson called a monster because of his part in the massacre at Red River. I looked over the lake toward our camp site on the island. Louis Primeau must have seen the same sparkle on the water, must have stood where we were and watched the great canoes come toward the portage. This country was home to him long before official discovery, and well traveled by the men who had guided the great explorers to their goals.

By the time we returned to the portage, Angélique was out tending a pot over the fire. I noticed immediately that the little bag of food had disappeared. Moody went over and talked to her for a moment in Cree. She left the fire, stepped into the tent, came out with a fresh roll of birchbark and sat down on the ground. Folding a square of bark much as white children used to fold squares of paper to cut out designs from the center, she began to chew. When she had finished, she unfolded the little square and showed us the pattern she had created. Not until each of us had a sample of her art did she put the roll away, but as a special demonstration and to show it was not as easy as it looked, she chewed one more, a surprising likeness of Tony and me in a canoe, even to the shape of my battered old hat. She also brought out three beautiful bannocks she had made that morning, and when we admired them she flashed us a big smile.

Moody told us about the Mamaygwessey, the little men with round heads, no noses, long spidery arms and legs with six fingers and six toes, whose likenesses we had seen among the pictographs of Black Bear Island Lake.

"These little creatures," he explained, "live usually in the rocks of rapids and when canoes come through, they delight in grasping the paddles or gunwales and when a canoe tips over, their shrieks of delight can be heard above the noise of the rapids."

When we told him what happened to our canoe on Dipper Lake, how it had blown off a rock without a trace or taking any water, he laughed loud and long.

"That's exactly the way they would do it," he said. "Not a sound or a mark anywhere. And you can be sure they saw to it that the canoe didn't smash itself to pieces against the cliff, but bounced around against those willows. You see there's no real mischief in their antics, just good clean fun."

He told us that Angélique was well acquainted with the Mamaygwessey, the dream people of the Crees, but would not talk about them with strangers.

From that moment on, the Mamaygwessey went with us, and whenever anything happened we could not quite explain, we knew they were responsible. Here again were the gremlins and elves, the dwarfs and fairies, and the little people of other lands as well—part of the legendry of all races on earth.

We threw on the canoes and packs, bade our friends good-by, and took off over the famous carry, "de Traite," the Frog Skin Portage of the Indians. We made it to the far end without a rest, loaded up once more, and proceeded down the new river system known as the Sturgeon Weir. That day the dream people were with us, and the birchbark designs made by Angélique were in our packs.

We reached Wood Lake after traversing the low swampy country of the upper Sturgeon Weir. The lake was one of the most attractive we had seen, again smooth glaciated islands, clean wooded shores all high and dry with many inviting camp sites. Traveling steadily southeast, we would reach the end of the lake about sunset, and if lucky we might find a view of the west on one of the last points or islands. As we neared the end of the lake, there was not a single place with an unobstructed view, so we finally chose a camp site behind a little point. We would have reflections there and some color, but miss the grand climax of the sun dropping below the horizon.

While setting up the tents and getting the fire under way,

we heard a canoe coming down the lake. Harry Moody had mentioned the possibility of visiting a prospector friend of his camped somewhere near the far end. We thought of paddling out and intercepting him, but our little camp site was far too small to hold his outfit, too. The motor droned off to the left a mile away, then sputtered to a stop.

It was then we talked for the first time of changing our plans and going on to the historic post of Cumberland House instead of ending at Flin Flon as originally planned. In good shape, we were traveling swiftly; the current would be with us and with luck the wind might hold in the northwest over the big lakes. It seemed far better to end up as the voyageurs used to do at the post, which was two days' travel beyond.

"I like the idea of ending at Cumberland," said Eric; "winds up the expedition as it should."

"It will make our route about five hundred miles instead of four hundred and fifty," said Omond. "Five hundred is a good round figure."

"Leave it to the Bourgeois," said Tony finally. "Whatever he decides, that we shall do."

The next morning after a swim, we packed up and headed toward the portages of the Three Rapids, which we found without difficulty. They were all short and fitted up with pole ramps and rollways for the big motor-driven freighters. We knew we were approaching the final Indian settlement of the trip and that soon we would see fishing camps again and trading posts. They were part of the picture of traveling down the ancient wilderness highway of the Churchill and the Sturgeon Weir.

At Medicine Rapids, Harry Moody was waiting to take our picture as we came through. A treacherous bit of water with a bad side sweep, it might have been hazardous had we taken it the wrong way. Angélique and William stood behind him, expectant and laughing, wondering how the white men would make it. Just above the riffle we had seen some paintings, another place where Indians offered something for good luck. We had nothing left to give, which explained perhaps why Omond and Denis ran into a rock, much to Angélique's delight. There was no damage, fortunately, except to their pride.

As we approached Pelican Narrows, a motor-driven canoe left the village, roared out from shore, circled us once, and then guided us grandly to the landing, which was crowded with Indians. It was a courteous gesture, and we were impressed. But we soon discovered the excitement at the village was not because of us. It was due to the fact that the Anglican bishop was coming in for a service.

As we paddled by the church, we saw two rows of brightly colored pennants extending all the way from the end of the dock to the doorway. A crowd of children dressed in their Sunday best were down at the water front. Scrubbed and combed, dressed in clean shirts and trousers or dresses and beaded moccasins, they waved and watched us approvingly. We, too, had come in from the bush to see the bishop.

At the Hudson's Bay Company dock just beyond, we were met by the young clerk, David La Riviere. He was dressed in a black suit, white shirt and a bright red tie, all in honor of the bishop. It was here I met Chief Linklater of the Pelican Narrows band of Crees. Years ago, back in the Quetico-Superior country, I had come to know a Jack Linklater, one of the finest woodsmen in the border regions. Jack's father was a hard-bitten Scotch factor at one of the posts in North Dakota, and his mother was a Cree. He had asked me to go with him to visit his mother's people, but something had always interfered. Now I knew this was the country he wanted me to see. No one here knew anything about Jack, but I could see a strong family resemblance, the same bold features, good eyes with a flash of humor.

Harry Moody had preceded us, and we found him in a little back room of the post, poring over some old maps. Angélique and William, he told us, had wanted to come in, for all their friends for many miles around would be here to greet the bishop.

"I might see you again, tomorrow," he said, "but my companions may not be able to go with me, due to social engagements."

After purchasing the few items needed, we stood outside the post watching the final preparations. Everyone was heading for the church dock and the landing ramp. Children running everywhere, and there was a sense of expectancy over the entire scene.

A breeze came up, and the colored pennants bordering the

dock and the path fluttered bravely. Then came the sound of the seaplane. With a grand roar it buzzed the village, headed up-wind, and taxied to the dock. Many hands tied it fast. There was not a sound; the great moment had come. The door of the plane opened, the pilot jumped out onto a pontoon, and the awesome figure of the bishop emerged. He stood on the dock, raised his hand in blessing, then went slowly up the walk toward the wide-open doors, followed by his flock. The church bell pealed, the flags fluttered, and soon through the open windows could be heard the solemn drone of the service.

We got into our canoes with not a soul to bid us good-by and paddled off toward the east. A husky howled long and mournfully as we slipped away. Soon the village was behind us—the cabins, the tents, the drying racks and the dogs tethered along the shore. We moved swiftly, for the current in the narrows was strong. Before us was the broad and quiet sweep of Mirond. We paused for a moment at the entrance and looked down the full length of it. Tonight, I thought, somewhere at the far end we would find the sunset camp I had dreamed about, a camp looking down the whole expanse of waterway, thirteen miles of it without a break. There we would know what a real sunset could be, a sunset in the calm with double shorelines and unbroken reflections. This was a night I had waited for.

For two hours we pushed down the lake. Then I began watching for an island or a point with a smooth rock facing the west. After about ten miles, I saw something that was a possibility, a glaciated spit of an island with a low shelf for a landing, with gnarled little pines and spruces in back. There we would land, set up the outfit, and look to our hearts' content.

It was so calm that the canoes seemed to be floating above the water, their reflections as real as the crafts themselves. The shores and islands were double and the flat spit of rock ahead lay like a great spear in the water. A few gulls careened overhead, and loon calls echoed against the hills. A great golden silence lay over the lake. We unconsciously watched our paddles so they would not strike the gunwales and break the spell.

As we approached our objective, I saw the landing was as perfect as I had hoped. Denis and I built a fireplace on a flat ledge near the water, while the others searched for tent sites. Sometime later they returned and reported the tents were all on the far side of the island because of the slope and roughness of the crest.

By now the sun was trembling on the horizon. Suddenly the west was all aglow toward Pelican Narrows. The bishop was gone now and the little flags hung limply from their poles, but the great day was far from over. There would be feasting and visiting far into the night. Harry Moody was no doubt still poring over his maps, Angélique and William making the rounds. All this seemed very far away and almost as unreal as the lakes, the rapids, and the storms we had come through. On Mirond at that moment time stood still.

CHAPTER 17

THE STURGEON WEIR

STARTED *at day break and pro-
ceeded up Rivierre Mal-in* [Maligne], *very appropriately named
as it is a continual Rapid for about thirty miles, the poles in use
nearly the whole way. Gummed at the entrance of Beaver*
[Amisk] *Lake where we found Mr. Dears with the Lesser Slave
Lake Canoes, and part of the N.W. Brigade, had some conversa-
tion with their people, and could have had several Deserters, they
appear much dissatisfied with their treatment at Lac la Pluie*
[Rainy Lake Post above Grand Portage]; *it appears there was a*

213

great scarcity of goods there, and the men could not get their full supplies of necessaries; passed through Beaver Lake, and encamped here at eight P.M.

—GEORGE SIMPSON (*1820*)

❧

WE AWAKENED to a stiff breeze out of the southeast and a rolling sea. I stood down at the landing remembering the calmness of the night before, the sunset, the reflections and the silence. Now all of that was gone and in a few hours there would be whitecaps. We would have to hurry if we were to make the far end of the lake and the mouth of the Sturgeon Weir.

Breakfast was simple and swift, a bowl of porridge and coffee. We packed hurriedly and were on the water at six thirty, dodging behind islands and points, fighting our way toward the protection of the far shore. By nine o'clock the waves were big. We knew what might happen by noon if the wind increased.

We worked our way to the southeast, and as we approached Corniele Portage we could see white spouts at the lower end of a rapids. We stopped to look them over just above it. A smooth slick ran down the center most of the way with heavy white water below. Tony and I started down. All went well until we hit the big waves. A huge swirling comber loomed before us and we bored into it; it broke over the bow and hit Tony squarely in the chest. We shipped water, wobbled free, rode the remaining waves to the rapids' end, then paddled ingloriously toward a flat, grassy bank to one side of the river. There we jumped into the stickiest glacial clay we had ever seen, tipped out the canoe and spent the next half hour cleaning the stuff off our boots, paddles and the canoe itself. Meanwhile, the others were far ahead, and we did not overtake them until we reached Dog Rapids at the true entrance of the river. We looked for a portage and found instead a channel of fast water going down through a dense growth of willows —a tiny run just wide enough for a canoe. It was impossible to see where it led, but I knew the flow would eventually take us into the open. We eased ourselves down cautiously, holding onto branches and guiding the canoe by hand rather than with our paddles. At one place, because of rocks, Tony went over the side and waded, holding onto the bow. He hopped in again just before the creek entered the main channel. The others seeing us go down in such unconventional fashion followed suit, but they were not as lucky as we. Omond and Denis hit a sharp rock and punched a small hole in the canvas, the first for them.

"This would have to happen in a little trickle like this," said Omond. "After all the big rocks, the rib-breakers of respectable rapids, not a hole until this baby rivulet."

Before us was the Sturgeon Weir, the river the Indians feared. No sooner had we entered the open water than we ran into the wind again, and in spite of the current we had to fight for headway. The river at this point was majestic, high rocky banks covered with jack pine and spruce, the channel a quarter of a mile wide running due south toward Birch Rapids ten miles away. We had been moving southeast for three days since crossing Frog Skin Portage, covering about sixty miles.

Tony and Omond were at our left, getting what protection they could from the lee bank. They stopped paddling. Omond raised his arm and pointed toward the shore.

There was a moose, belly-deep in the shallow water of a little bay. It was the first we had seen, proof that there was little travel on the Weir. The other canoe came up, and we sat there watching the animal feed. The moose was as huge as a horse and black against the bright green rushes in the shallows. It munched calmly on some lily roots, the long stems dripping from its mouth. As soon as its head went under water, we paddled forward, and when it emerged with another dripping mouthful we stopped dead once more.

According to David Thompson: "The flesh of a moose in good condition contains more nourishment than that of any other Deer; five pounds of this meat being held equal in nourishment to seven pounds of any other meat even of the Bison, but for this it must be killed where it is quietly feeding. . . . The nose of the Moose, which is very large and soft is accounted a great delicacy. It is very rich meat. The bones of its legs are very hard and several things can be made of them. His skin makes the best of leather. It is the noblest animal of the Forest, and the richest prize the Hunter can take."

Though the light was bad, Denis groped for his camera and took one swift shot.

Suddenly the animal noticed us, stopped chewing, then almost imperceptibly moved toward the bank. Upon reaching firm footing, it exploded in a cascade of mud and water, then faded into the spruces and was gone.

"We could have taken him alive," said Tony. "One more rush and we could have had him."

"Once long ago," I told them, "I paddled up to a big bull on Swampy Bay of Sturgeon Lake in the Quetico, got so close I slapped him across the rump with my paddle."

"Yes?" queried Denis.

"It went right up into the air and almost fell backward in my lap."

"Bourgeois," said Omond, "you must have been young then and very foolish."

"That is true," I replied, "young and foolish enough to even dream of riding one."

The river narrowed and quickened ahead, and we sailed through the gap without losing position or even changing stroke. Just below, we stopped on a flat rocky island for lunch.

Omond got out the maps and checked them. "I was right," he announced. "We're on the fifty-fifth parallel and with luck we should be well into Amisk or Beaver Lake by tonight."

None of us made any comment, but we knew that rapids not on the maps lay ahead. Anyone of them could mean running, lining, or portaging, possibly all three. The Indians must have reason for their feelings about the Sturgeon Weir.

A few hours later we found ourselves approaching Birch

Rapids. The portage looked used, the grass beaten down at its start. That told us what to do, and we landed above on a slippery bank of clay. As we started over, Tony slipped and went down with the canoe on top of him. The recent rains had not improved the trail and in places the footing was treacherous. We crossed without further mishap, however, sliding down slopes, grasping trees and bushes desperately. After we had loaded and pushed off again, we turned as always, looked back up the rapids around which we had come and were glad we had not run them.

Beyond Birch and before Lake Maligne the wind veered completely around and the sun was gone, the sky full of racing black clouds with flashes of lightning between them. Maligne was well named for us—rapids shouting ahead, lightning and thunder, and wild gusts of wind from every point of the compass. Then it was deadly calm, and we sat there somewhat cowed, debating whether to go on or to look for shelter while there was time. All of us had had enough experience to sense that evil was brewing; such sudden calm and uncertain gales meant violence. We looked over the shores but they were nothing but swamp—not a high bank or a sign of a rocky shelf, one of those soggy places we always avoided. There was nothing we could do but push on in the hope of finding higher ground before the storm broke. It was a bad decision, for within minutes the sky grew almost black and rain began to fall. Hastily we got out the ponchos, covered the packs, then pushed into the willows as far as we could and sat there waiting for the storm to break.

The sky became darker and darker and flashes of lightning burned their way across it. Rolling peals of thunder added the final touch. Ducks flew madly up and down the river; an osprey flew with them, too concerned to think of them as prey. This would have been a beautiful thing to watch from the safety of a snug cabin, but from a canoe in the flooded willows with the river heaving beneath us, it was far from comfortable. A bolt of lightning hit a stub so close to shore we could smell it and feel the tension in the air. The storm was more violent than anything we had ever experienced in the Rainy Lake country or anywhere else.

The land had been well named. It was the weather breeder of Canada. From it came powerful winds and unpredictable storms—violent and short-lived it is true, but all the more vicious because of their suddenness. A man might do well to watch the skies and take cover at the slightest hint of danger. We sat there for an hour and then pulled out of the willows and headed downstream. The wind died as suddenly as it had come. The rain continued just enough to build up the slosh in the bottom of the canoes. Our packs were getting wet and it was late, but the shores ahead looked unpromising. There was no high country in sight. For once it looked as though we would have to forget the luxury of clean rocks and make an Indian camp back on the muskeg. We slogged through the rain, watching hopefully for any rise of ground, and finally passed through a narrows where the current was more perceptible. Gradually it grew swifter, then we heard the sound we had been waiting for, the roar of another rapids—Leaf of the Sturgeon Weir. None of us had forgotten the first Leaf and what had happened there, and we wondered if this might be a repetition.

"There might be a rock below the rapids," said Tony cheerfully, "and if there is I will catch some walleyes for supper."

That was plausible enough. If the rapids were as bad as they sounded, there would have to be a portage and possibly a ledge. We pushed on toward the roar, and Tony and I explored the bank above. There was the trail. To our amazement, it was as white as a trail in the winter, covered completely with hailstones as big as marbles. At least we missed that part of the storm.

We landed and found a fairly level spot for a camp site halfway across, dropped our packs there, but because the approach was muddy, decided to go to the end and see what it was like. Perhaps, I thought, Tony was right and we would find a smooth rock there and he could catch some fish for supper. The trail was old and we immediately saw why, with the river boiling down through the fringe of trees. But the end of it was as muddy as its beginning—certainly no incentive to camp. We went back and upon reaching the landing saw the other canoes had put in a hundred yards above on a narrow shelf of rock. We retrieved our packs and paddled over. The shelf wasn't much, barely room for the tents, but it was high and dry and close to the water.

Just as we got there the sun came out and shone on the rock, and we were happy with our good fortune. The tents were pitched facing the water with the fireplace in front of them, the canoes to one side. We were on the Sturgeon Weir and had come through what the voyageurs called the Maligne. As I cooked supper I thought of the Maligne River in the Quetico-Superior, a boiling stream with rapids and high, timbered shores, and of the other Malignes I had known in the country they had explored. It was a high-sounding, wonderful name for lakes and rivers on days such as the one we had just known. And what a day it had been: six white pelicans gliding across the black curtain of the storm, an osprey fleeing in panic with the ducks, moose wallows along the marshy shores, the almost complete abandonment by the Crees of the route over which we had come.

The ration of rum that night was more than welcome. We were wet and had been cold most of the day. We sat there watching the sun dodge through the swiftly disappearing storm clouds, listening to the roar of Leaf Rapids, wondering about Scoop coming up and all the fast water that was not on the map at all. We talked again about the possibility of going on to Cumberland House instead of ending at Flin Flon and taking a truck from there cross-country to The Pas.

"From Cumberland House," said Elliot, "we can get an Indian to take us down the Saskatchewan in a big canoe with a motor to The Pas. We can make the ninety miles in half a day and catch our plane on schedule for Winnipeg from there."

"Fifty miles more if we do that," said Omond checking his

maps. "With luck and no storms and running a lot of fast water we can do it."

The decision was clear. We would all rather follow the historic trade route to Cumberland House than end up at the mining town of Flin Flon. We wanted the challenge of those miles and an excuse to postpone the end of the trip as long as possible. We were becoming increasingly aware of the passage of time and the day when we would have to put the canoes away in some warehouse, check the packs, sort out the duffle, have a final meal in some restaurant, and then at last stand in line at an airport waiting to be checked in. All of a sudden the Sturgeon Weir became very important to us. If we followed the new plan, we would merely pass through Amisk Lake with the mining camp of Flin Flon lying in the distance, go across, find its outlet, continue once more down the Weir to Namew or Sturgeon and finally to Cumberland House, the oldest Hudson's Bay Post in the Northwest.

"Funny," said Eric, "none of us ever thought of this before. There never should have been any question."

An Indian had told us at Pelican Rapids that there were thirty miles of fast water on the lower Sturgeon Weir, but that didn't worry us. We were going through to Cumberland House.

The sunset was a gorgeous one—flaming streams of color against the last wisps of clouds. Ducks whispered overhead, and the air was alive with the sound of the rapids below.

Omond came over and stood with me down at the water's edge.

"What do you think?" he asked. "How does it look for tomorrow?"

"With that sunset," I answered, "it's bound to be fair. We've had our rain for a while."

"Good night," he said. "I hope you're right."

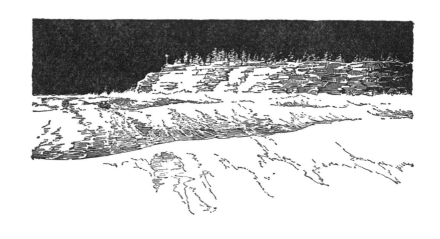

CHAPTER 18

THE RED CLIFFS OF AMISK

HE *Sturgeon Weir River dis-charges itself into this lake, and its bed seems to be of the same kind of rock, and is almost a continual rapid. Its direct course is almost west by north, and with its windings is about thirty miles. It takes its waters into Beaver Lake [Amisk], the southwest side of which consists of the same rock lying in thin strata; the route then proceeds from island to island for about twelve miles, and along the north shore, for four miles more, the whole being a northwest course to the entrance of the river in latitude 54.32. North.*

—ALEXANDER MACKENZIE

224

THE NEXT MORNING we awakened to the drum of rain on our tents. The wind had been from the west, blowing directly into our shelters, and the ends of the sleeping bags were drenched. I leaned over and felt mine, then Tony's. Both were sodden and heavy. They would have to dry for a long time in sun and wind before they would be light and fluffy again. Slipping on my rain shirt, I went outside to start the fire, but every time a blaze started the wind and rain put it out. After many tries I succeeded, and when the coffee had come to a boil and the mush was cooked, I called the rest. We sat there in the shelter of the Baker-tent fly, no one saying much except Tony.

"Did you notice, Bourgeois," he asked me in his delectable accent, "those poodles in the tent?"

It was just what we needed. "We had the biggest poodles," said Elliot laughing, "a whole litter of them from one end of the tent to the other."

Only Eric had escaped, for he had been able to pitch his little tent at enough of an angle to the shelf to miss the rain.

It seemed foolhardy to start out in such weather, and we waited hopefully for a break that never came. Finally we packed the wet tents, the soggy bags, and the outfit into the canoes and drifted down toward the portage.

In the rain, Leaf Rapids sounded even louder than the night before. The landing was slippery and the portage still white with hailstones. In the hollows were mounds of them, and we scooped them up with our hands. Slipping and sliding, trying to watch our footing, we made the carry without mishap, loaded the canoes once more, and headed down toward Scoop Rapids. There, according to the Crees, travelers could always dip out a fish from a shallow pool at the lower end. Someone long ago, they said, had left a scoop net there for that purpose, each user leaving it in the same place for the next one coming through. We did not find the scoop, nor did we locate the pool, for the rapids were roaring and high and the fishing place covered by the flood.

"Perhaps," said Denis, "the little men have taken it away, the ones with no noses."

It was there we met Conservation Officer Charley Salt camped all alone at the portage's upper end, high above the landing. He had come up the river with his motor, told us of a broken Grumman canoe below Snake Rapids, advised us strongly not to try running them. A husky young lad from eastern Ontario, he had taken to the bush as naturally as an Indian. Broad of shoulder, with flashing white teeth, an open face and a shock of long blond hair, he looked like a Viking. His neat little tent was pitched tight as a fiddlestring, and his whole outfit was spanking new and clean.

To Charley Salt, traveling alone to Pelican Rapids, the North was still all romance and excitement, every difficulty a challenge, every hardship savored to the full. We watched him pack and head toward Leaf and the Maligne, caught his gay wave as he disappeared around the bend.

Beyond Scoop there was swamp again, with a profusion of

bird life. We passed an Indian cemetery on the north bank of the river and saw several lob pines marking the course and its many turns. Lob pines are the original trail markers of voyageur days. Picking a spruce or small pine on some high ridge or promontory, voyageurs stripped branches from the lower part of the tree, leaving a tuft or broom on top. Sometimes they merely cut a section from beneath the tip. But whatever the method employed, such a tree could be seen for long distances. Travelers accustomed to watching the skyline with its evenly pinnacled fringe of spruce would notice immediately any discrepancy. In the old days lob pines marked the canoe routes from Montreal into the far Northwest. It was good to see them again, to realize there were still places where such old traditions survive, even in the jet age.

As we paddled along I thought of what Charley Salt had said about the new fish-filleting plant at Pelican Narrows. Planes were coming in daily during the fishing season to fly the fillets to Winnipeg for shipment to the East. A new wave of prosperity was dawning for the Indians, and their old way of life was changing fast. As I watched a lone lob pine on the horizon, I wondered if the changes would bring as much happiness as he thought.

Signs of beaver were plentiful, indicating there was little trapping on the river. Along the Churchill there had been none at all, except up tributary creeks; now there was evidence everywhere. Whitened sticks of gnawed aspen floated along the shore. There were signs on trails and canals leading inland. Flattened sedges showed where they had been. Perhaps, I thought, the fishing industry was keeping trappers close at home, resulting in the abandonment of ancient trapping grounds. In time, perhaps, the beaver might even move close to the villages, if no one was interested in the hard work of taking them.

All that day, beavers were with us. It seemed right to be in beaver country again, for of all forms of life in the Northwest, this animal was responsible for exploration and trade. A beaver skin was standard currency and all articles of trade were evaluated by the number of skins they would bring.

A Moose Fort Record of 1784 gave a few comparative trading values.

Arrowheads	9	1 Beaver
Awl blades	12	1 "
Bayonets	2	1 "
Beads	1 #	2 "
Bells hawk	8 prs.	1 "
Blankets	1 point	1 "
Blankets	2 points	2 ½ "
Blankets	3 points	4 "
Boxes tobacco	2	1 "
Brandy	1 Gns	4 "
Buttons	12 doz.	1 "
Cloth	1 yd	2 "
Chizzels	2	1 "
Combs	2	1 "
Flints	20	1 "

Guns	4 ft	12 Beaver
Shot	5 #	1 "
Gunpowder	2 Horns	1 "
Kettles	1 #	1 "
Shirts check	1	1 "
Spoons	4	1 "
Knives	8	1 "
Stockings	1 pr	1 ¼ "

The beaver skin was the standard in evaluating all other furs. It took two of the hides to be worth as much as one wolverine, three for a bear, one for twenty rabbits, 4 mink, or 10 pounds of goose feathers. The beaver was king for almost three hundred years. Today it is revered as a symbol in all of Canada.

While we were paddling by the mouth of a little creek a beaver appeared, swimming across the opening with a leafy branch of aspen in its mouth. When it saw the canoe it raised its tail and with a mighty whack warned all members of the colony to beware.

A little farther on was a house close to the shore, a live house with much activity around it. The beavers were laying in their winter's supply of food and had already sunk a considerable amount of brush, aspen, birch, alder, and willow. Before long the fall storms would come, followed by the swift freezing of all lakes and rivers. Then for six months they would subsist on what they had stored.

"Dose beavaire," said Denis, "she is a mighty fine aneemahl."

Several hours later we approached Snake Rapids Portage, one of the longest we would encounter on our trip down the Weir. We found it immediately, traveled the three quarters of a mile without the usual rests, found at its end the broken aluminum canoe Charley had told us about. It had gone down the rapids, been wedged between two rocks and torn apart by the force of the current. Whose it was or whether or not its owners had come through alive, we did not know. Someone had hauled it onto the rocks and left it there as a reminder of what can happen. We stood around it, looking it over, all of us thinking the same thing. This might well have been one of our Peterboroughs, but the story would then have been different; instead of a torn and twisted piece of metal it would have been a splintered wreck of cedar, spruce, and canvas.

At such a place, where someone had probably drowned, the voyageurs would have erected crosses. Daniel Harmon on an expedition in 1800 out of Montreal toward the West spoke of the effect these markers had on him. Passing Roche Capitaine Portage, he said:

"This portage is so named from a large rock, that rises to a considerable height above the water in the middle of the rapid. During the day, we have come up several difficult ones, where many persons have been drowned, either in coming up or going down. For every such unfortunate person, whether his corpse is found or not, a cross is erected by his companions, agreeably to a custom of the Roman Catholics; and at this place, I see no less than fourteen. This is a melancholy sight. It leads me to reflect on the folly and temerity of man, which causes him to press on in the path, that has conducted so many of his fellow creatures prematurely to the grave. . . .

"The Canadian Voyageurs, when they leave one stream to go up or down another, have a custom of pulling off their hats, and making the sign of the cross, upon which one in each canoe, or at least, in each brigade repeats a short prayer. The same ceremonies are observed by them, whenever they pass a place where someone has been interred, and a cross erected. Those therefore who are in the habit of voyaging this way, are obliged to say their prayers more frequently perhaps than when at home; for at almost every rapid which we have passed, since we left Montreal, we have seen a number of crosses erected; and at one I counted no less than thirty. . . . With such dismal spectacles, however, almost continually before our eyes, we press forward, with all the ardor and rashness of youth, in the same dangerous path, stimulated by the hopes of gratifying the eye and of securing a little gold."

Toward sunset we were at the final rapids above Amisk Lake. This, according to the map, was Spruce, and we looked them over carefully, remembering the Grumman. It was getting late and the channel was far from reassuring, so we decided to be prudent, make the portage and reach Amisk without accident. There we would surely find a good camp site on some island or point. Salt had mentioned several old Indian shacks or "cabooses" as he called them at the opening of the river, but as we approached and saw their dank and swampy situation we gave up the idea of sleeping under a roof and headed for the big water instead.

As we passed beyond the fringing rushes of the river's outlet, there was an open horizon and, several miles across, a long point with limestone cliffs blazing in the level rays of the setting sun. It was as though a great brush had streaked it with Chinese red. Off the Shield once more and before us was the horizontal limestone of another geological era, limestone evidently covered with the same orange lichens we had seen at our second camp on Shangwenaw, transformed again by the blazing sun.

We sat there in our canoes, conscious of the whitecaps out in the open. While it was perfectly calm where we were, half a mile from shore and toward the cliffs a gale was having its way. We must quickly decide either to camp where we were, hug the right shore and travel much farther to reach the outlet, or take advantage of the northwest wind and sail across in an hour.

After all the big water we had been through—Dead Lake, Mirond, and Ile à la Crosse—I knew we could make it. The Peterboroughs could take this one as they had taken blows many times before without shipping so much as a drop; we were seasoned canoemen and knew the score. We would have to work our way around the end of a long point and its shining spray-tossed cliffs and find shelter behind it. Within an hour it would be dusk, but that last hour would be a beautiful one with the wind all but hurling us toward our goal. It was too good a chance to miss, too exciting a challenge to forego.

The canoes came together in the swampy lee of the river's opening and we debated our course. I sensed the voyageurs all felt as I did, confident and sure. The cliffs were flaming brighter than ever. There was no resisting them now.

Omond looked at me. "Bourgeois," he said, "it's up to you."

I looked toward the cliffs once more and the wave-tossed miles in between.

"Let's go," I said, and without more ado we headed out into the open.

The canoes were well spaced but close enough so we would not lose touch. As the distance from the shore increased, we began to feel the wind and were soon in the grip of it, coasting the broad rollers toward the red cliffs.

The wind was steady and the farther out we got the stronger it became, pushing like a great hand on our backs. Hissing combers were around us and it was every canoe for itself, no chance even for a side glance to see what was happening to the others. Carefully quartering to the southeast and toward the end of the point, I was conscious of each wave, judging its power and lift by the sharpness of the approaching hiss. If we skirted the point too close we might hit submerged rocks, if we went out too far we could be carried out into the open lake with its twelve-mile sweep and miss our chance of turning into the shelter behind it.

The cliffs were still a couple of miles away. Only the tip of the point was flaming, the base a dull, angry red fading into the blackness toward the west. The canoe would ride a great roller, slip off its crest, and in that moment of cascading down the slope of the trough we would start quartering. In the blow on Dead Lake the sun had been shining, the combers sparkling and alive. Now in the near dusk they were dull and gray, the valleys in between, bottomless and black. Like running a rapids in poor light, you depended on the feel of things.

Every third or fourth wave was bigger than the rest and I could sense its lift long before it struck. When it caught us the canoe would rise swiftly, then hurtle forward like a great gray spear into the spray. The cliffs were much closer now, their lower parts brushed with black, only the top and very tip of the point still colored. All I could think of was a red knife sticking out into the blackness of the east, its tip alive, its blade and handle darkening into purple. We were quartering successfully and would miss the stiletto's end, but what was in its lee we did not know. Could we land there, or would we find the same precipitous cliffs we faced? We would have to camp there even if we had to climb clear to their tops.

As we drew near, the roar of crashing waves was deafening. Great blocks of limestone lay out in the water below the cliffs with spray dashing high around them. I headed our canoe toward a point a hundred yards beyond the farthest rock lying off the end of the point. Then exactly as we had planned and hoped, we were slipping smoothly by. At that moment there was a slight lull in the wind. I turned the canoe sharply and we were coasting along a calm and beautiful shore covered with flat horizontal slabs of rock backed by huge trees.

In the lee of a limestone block that lay just inside the tip of the point we had a good view of the entire shore. We picked a flat place a few hundred yards below and landed, hauled the canoes out of danger, and found level spots for the tents under big spreading spruces nearby. Denis and I built a fire-place and a patio out of slabs of yellow limestone. There was an abundance of dry wood, and a fire was soon burning and supper under way.

We had found a strange new land. The trees behind us were entirely different from the aspen, spruce, and birch we had known all the way down the Churchill and the Weir. We were off the Shield again and were now on a sedimentary formation that extended far toward Athabasca and the Mac-kenzie.

Omond fixed a special brew that night and a surprise, some hoarded nuts. We drank to our luck in finding an-other beautiful camp site and to the red cliffs of Amisk. As we sat there quietly in the dusk listening to the gale roaring harmlessly overhead and the heavy crash of combers off the point, there was little to say about what we had done. But none of us would ever forget the glory of those cliffs flaming in the last rays of the sun, the wind-washed waves with their foaming crests, the sense of being hurled across those miles toward an uncertain goal, and then the calm, with the shout-ing all behind us.

As I sat there I thought of Al Kennedy, an old prospector friend of mine, who thirty years before had wanted me to come here with him to look for gold. He had been in the rush of the year before and returned with fabulous stories of nuggets and moose and Indian tribes. I was young then and had listened with wide-eyed wonder. Flin Flon—the very sound of it meant adventure. But I did not go after all and stayed in the Quetico-Superior country and the land of the Hudson Bay watershed. I often wondered what might have happened had it been otherwise. Would I have found the gold, or would I have been just another bushwhacker roaming the wilds and searching for the elusive mother lode? We were now within a few miles of Flin Flon, but I would not see it after all.

The Chinese red of the cliffs across the lake was almost gone, fading to mahogany, and the waves were wine and black. Only those close in showed glistening crests. A long slow wash of surf came into our bay. Tomorrow with the wind down, we could cross the open stretch before us, head down the final reaches of the Sturgeon Weir toward Namew and then to Cumberland House where we would say good-by to the canoes, pack our outfit for the last time and go down the great Saskatchewan to The Pas.

CHAPTER 19

GOOSE CREEK CAMP

TARTED *at four O'Clock* A.M., *the three Light Canoes in Company detained at the entrance of the Grand Traverse* [Namew] *from twelve till four by adverse wind and encamped on the Rat Portage* [Goose Creek Camp] *at nine* P.M., *here we found at the further end a N.W. Half loaded Canoe for Lesser Slave Lake, passengers Mr. Henry and one Primeau* [a Monster], *who made himself very conspicuous in the Red River Massacre; this fellows name is in several warrants, but we have none in our possession otherways he would have been secured.*

—GEORGE SIMPSON (*1820*)

237

꽃

UP WITH THE SUN and away to an early start, we were heading for the lichen-covered cliffs across the bay and the entrance to the lower reaches of the Sturgeon Weir on the way to Namew. The cliffs were gray, stark and bold above the calmness of the water. It was hard to remember the waves in the lazy swells that remained, the dashing spray and the excitement of a few hours before. We coasted the shore toward the river's mouth. This was the part the Indians had warned us about—rapids, rapids, rapids, none of them with portages.

"One place," said an Indian at Pelican, "many miles of bad water. My people go there long time ago."

If the river was too impassable to bother maintaining portages, I thought, it must be rough indeed and like all other difficult routes would be abandoned in time. Perhaps that was the reason we had seen few Indians since starting down the Weir.

We passed Sturgeon and Warburton bays, caught at last a haze lying to the north—smoke from the mines of Flin Flon beyond the islands and up the east channel. The haze was like fog far in the distance. It was easy to imagine it was only mist coming out of the channel, hard to believe that a few miles away was a modern town with an airfield and a road leading to The Pas.

We were now in the river mouth with the great body of Amisk Lake behind us. The water was crystal clear in contrast to the darkness of the Churchill and the upper reaches of the

Weir. Flowing over limestone, it was as transparent as the chalk streams of England, and little did we know how much its clarity would mean in the miles ahead.

We looked over the first white water, decided not to shoot, and made a long involved portage instead. From that point, however, we encountered the most delightful series of runnable rapids we had known, the water so clear we could actually see its bottom and the rocks ahead, could guide by sight instead of feel. We learned more about how a river behaves when it runs over rocks than ever before, how large a spout would come from a certain depth over a ledge, how swirls and whirlpools were shaped and how to take them. In dark water a swirl might mean almost anything, but when you could see what caused it and exactly how it moved, adjustment of the canoe to its pull was simple. It was like slaloming down a good ski slope, zigzagging from one side of the river to the other, knowing exactly what was going to happen because of perfect visibility and control.

No canoeman could ever forget Sir William Butler's vivid description of running a rapids on the Winnipeg a hundred years ago. I thought of it as we sped down the Sturgeon Weir that day. Rapids do not change, nor do canoes or the men who man them.

"As the canoe—never appearing so frail and tiny as when it is about to commence its series of wild leaps and rushes— nears the rim where the waters disappear from view, the bowsman stands up and, stretching forward his head, peers down the eddying rush; in a second he is on his knees again;

without turning his head he speaks a word or two to those who are behind him; then the canoe is in the rim; she dips to it, shooting her bows clear out of the water and striking hard against the lower level. After that there is no time for thought; the eye is not quick enough to take in the rushing scene. There is a rock here and a big green cave of water there; there is a tumultous rising and sinking of snow-tipped waves; there are places that are smooth-running for a moment and then yawn and open up into great gurgling chasms the next; there are strange whirls and backward eddies and rocks, rough and smooth and polished—and through all this the canoe glances like an arrow, dips like a wild bird down the wing of a storm, now slanting from a rock, now edging a green cavern, now breaking through a backward rolling billow, without a word spoken, but with every now and again a quick convulsive twist and turn of the bow paddle to edge far off some rock, to put her full through some boiling billow, to hold her steady down the slope of some thundering chute which has the power of a thousand horses."

In several places we ran continuous rapids and fast water for miles at a time. What speed we made we did not know, but it was far swifter than the traditional three or four miles an hour of ordinary lake travel. None of the rapids ran through gorges, none of them were as wild and desperate as the one Sir William described, but the challenge was there even though the river had a smooth and steady descent over the relatively flat ledges of limestone.

It was a joy to see the canoes moving like dancers through intricate steps, weaving, backing, hesitating for a moment, only to dart forward again, thrusting and feinting at times like fencers testing their opponents. Bend after bend disappeared behind us. We stayed close to the bank around the turns, so if danger loomed we could head for the willows and get out, but not once during that entire stretch of river was it necessary.

Once Eric swung in close. "This was the river the Indians were afraid of," he yelled.

I tried to answer, but in a moment we were separated again and heading downstream as before.

As we neared the outlet of Goose Creek, however, we were forced to make a portage around a rapids that looked impossible. We were approaching Namew or Sturgeon Lake and the Cumberland country and from now on could expect to find signs of Indian travel. Here the river narrowed into a gorge and though we could still see the rocks and channels as clearly as before, there was no chance of shooting. As usual when confronted by a well-used Indian trail, we gave up any idea of running the river. If they portaged there was a good reason.

In mid-afternoon, as we made the portage, we thought of all the carries we had been saved through the co-operation of the river. To our delight, at the far end was a smooth ledge of rock, possibly an acre in extent, with a fine landing below the rapids' end. An old voyageurs' camp site, it was a spot that without question had been used for many years. Anyone going through on this particular route would remember it. A large party could camp there with ease.

It was good to have space and room to spread out and was exactly what we needed after the rains, the storms, and the spray of the last few days. Though still too early to stop, we decided to camp and spend an afternoon doing all the little chores that had been put off. We spread out sleeping bags, ponchos and tents, food bags and clothing in the full blaze of the sun. Every bush and tree was festooned. From a little distance one would think a large party of Crees had been living there for days.

We had earned this respite, and we would pull into Cumberland as voyageurs should, with gear in shape and everything under control. Damp and rain had taken their toll and telltale signs of mold were beginning to show. Our sleeping bags had never had a chance to recover from the drenching they got above Spruce Rapids and after the storm on the Maligne. Now all swayed in the sun and wind and Tony turned them over and over so no part would fail to dry.

"Look," he said proudly, "they are getting fluffy again." I felt them and saw that even half an hour had had its effect. That night they would be light and warm again, as bags of down should be.

Tony pitched our tent near a big spruce in the center of the little clearing. The Baker went up on the east side where the last rays of the sun would shine in and complete the drying. Eric pitched his pup tent on a little rise overlooking the rapids.

When all tents were up, the place felt like home. How swiftly this feeling comes on a camp site one has never seen before. Once shelter is made and the outfit has taken over the site, a fire is built and the canoes put away, any place becomes home and little things become as familiar as in a house one has lived in many years. This feeling of having many homes all through the wilderness gives a sense of belonging, as all know who have ever been there.

The tents made our camp seem like a little village. Instead of being hidden by brush and trees, for once they were out in the open. We walked around from tent to tent, visiting as though we were on a village square, the fireplace in the center being common ground. Greetings were gay, and every man did the innumerable little tasks that had to be done or simply amused himself with whatever took his fancy at the moment. Denis sat down in front of the Baker, got out his diary and began to write. Omond laid out his maps and studied them sagely. Eric busied himself constructing a convenience with a suitable view of the river. Tony went out to the point of a big rock and fished for walleyes and northern pike.

Elliot went prospecting for artifacts in the cracks of the rocks around the old fireplace, came up with pieces of willow-ware china, some brass buttons and bits of metal. What a treasure trove there must have been all around that ancient site, what hidden stories of the past, for the ledge had figured large in the plans of all expeditions on the Sturgeon Weir. On a river with marshy banks, a smooth flat rock such as this was something to remember. Within an easy day's travel to

Cumberland House when coming down from the Churchill or coming up from the post itself, it was a natural stopping place.

"We've come exactly 465 miles," said Omond. "Twenty-five or thirty more and we'll have approximately 500, not counting all of the side trips and the dodging behind islands and skirting bays."

"Say that again," said Denis.

"Four hundred sixty-five," repeated Omond. "Thirty to go."

Denis jotted down these vital statistics in his diary for the day, then snapped the covers shut.

"Bourgeois," he said, "it has been a grand trip."

Omond decided on this day, a very special day of thanksgiving and celebration, that we should have our ration of rum early, so he picked a smooth shelf overlooking the tail end of the rapids and laid out the ingredients with as meticulous care as though he was preparing for a banquet. By this time his activities toward the end of each day had assumed the significance of a ritual. The pot of water was put out, along with the fruit-juice crystals, the plastic bottle of rum, and the enamel cups.

I fussed around the fire, stewing a mess of beans and some dried fruit. One more camp, perhaps two, and we would be at Cumberland House. It became increasingly hard to realize that the trip was drawing to a close and that this was the end of many things for all of us. Tony might be transferred to some other post, maybe even Australia or the Far East. Omond might also move away to England, if events shaped up as they promised. The Army might change things for Elliot, too. Eric, Denis, and I were definitely hoping to keep on as we were, but even with us one could never be sure.

At the moment it seemed as though we had always been together, that our old life was nebulous and unreal. This way of existence, living in tents and traveling together each day, seemed the way life should be. We had shared wind and storm, rapids and portages, and all of that had been good. I would miss Tony with his talk of "poodles in the tent," of "calooses" on his hands, Omond's pondering over maps and aerial photographs, Eric's careful planning of details, Denis running around for rocks and firewood the instant we hit shore. And what would I do without Elliot's help around the cooking pots, should he ever have to say No to an expedition in the future?

I stirred the beans, tried bits of the salt pork floating around on top, added a pinch of salt and some pepper and a few last remnants from the bag of dehydrated onions, and tasted cautiously.

A pair of gray whisky-jacks hovered around the fire. This was as it should be. No old camp site was quite complete without them. They sat in a jack pine close by, and their soft warbling notes were good to hear. I tossed out some bits of old bannock and in an instant they were down at my feet, then off into the trees and back again. The chickadees came in with a flutter of tiny wings and the merry "chickadee dee dee" of their welcome. I found a tiny bag of salted sunflower seeds I had brought along on a whim, and though the birds had never seen any before, they knew exactly what to do with them. Holding the seed between their tiny feet, they pecked off the hull with a couple of deft strokes. The news spread and soon a dozen were around.

Elliot came over and watched them.

"Hungry little beggars," he said. Then he dug with a sharpened stick in a wide crack beside the fireplace and pulled out a great chunk of moss that had filled it. He laid it on a shelf of clean limestone and began to comb it carefully, picking it apart bit by bit. He was deeply absorbed and I knelt beside him and watched. There were half a dozen more fragments of the Hudson's Bay Company willowware packed in from York factory on the great Bay, a section of Indian crockery, the edge of an earthenware bowl, broken stems from the clay pipes of voyageurs, a brass button from a Canadian Army uniform of World War I—all of that from a single crevice.

"If I only had a shovel," he said, "think of what I might find. Every crack is full of stuff, every foot of ground around here packed with relics."

Elliot was a true archaeologist, never so happy as when looking for evidence of the past. He picked up his treasures, laid the collection in a neat row on Omond's ledge where all could see and admire.

"Come and get it," called Omond, and we left whatever we were doing and joined him at the ledge, looked at Elliot's findings, then sat there sipping our rum. We were content and happy and said little. We had said most of the things that needed saying, long ago.

I watched Tony sitting on the edge of the rock—Tony, who soon would be going back to the endless round of diplomatic functions. He sat looking over the end of the rapids, thinking only of the fish he had just taken.

Omond circled around, passing out some tidbits he had been saving for special occasions. I went back to stir the beans. They were about done and so was the fruit. I took the pail down and set it in the water to cool.

It got dark quickly there on the river bottom, and as soon as supper was over, the dishes washed and all the outfit stored safely away, we crawled into the tents, lay there for a moment listening to the roar of the rapids, the slow steady pulsation of moving water. I thought again of what the Indians had said about the Weir—"the last part all bad water"—and wondered if our luck would hold. But that was tomorrow, and tomorrow could wait. A flock of ducks flew over, and I could hear their wings as they headed toward the marshes above. Tony was breathing heavily. Over in the Baker I could hear Elliot. The camp was asleep.

CHAPTER 20

THE CHIMNEYS OF NAMEW

1790—Sept 13th Monday—at 7¼ AM *embarked at Cumberland House in company with Mr. Malcom Ross (with wife and two children) Peter Fidler my assistant, Hugh Lisk, Robert Garroch, Malcom Grot, and Peter Brown in two Canoes, all except myself and Peter Fidler being supplied with some Scotch Barley, Oatmeal, Flour and Salt, myself and Peter Fidler having only about 30 pounds of Flour and none of the other articles, an Indian which I had kept in the summer for the purpose of piloting us part of the way being gone ahead. . . . [After passing through Cumberland House Lake,] a large part of the lake then opens called by the Indians Nemew or limestone Lake.*

Sept 14th Tuesday—5¼ AM got underway entered Nemew Kip-pa-ha-gan Seepee or Sturgeon wear river . . . passed the mouth of a small river running out of a lake in the port nelson track called Goose Lake, and came to a fall carried 195 yards on north side good carrying place and put up at 9½ AM found two Canadians at this place waiting for canoes coming up with goods . . . and five tents of Indians . . . all of them desirous to have us go to their country.

—PHILIP TURNOR

WE LEFT our camp at Rat Portage with regret. During our stay we had become fond of the flat limestone ledges of the Athabasca formation. How strange they were compared to the granites of the Shield. Laid down by an arm of the sea millions of years ago, they spoke of a different era. In such a formation were the oil-bearing deposits of the Athabasca and the Mackenzie, the sands that would some day mean the opening of great expanses of wilderness to the west. Experts said that along the Athabasca River were three hundred billion barrels of oil in one concentrated formation of saturated sand, enough to supply the needs of the continent for over a century to come. But far more important to us was the memory of what a single ledge of it had meant to a tired party of voyageurs in need of rest.

Again we traveled the river as we had the day before, careening down smoothly, sometimes shooting clear across to avoid an obstruction far ahead. When we neared the river's mouth we could see the open horizon of Namew. A shelf ran across from bank to bank, the spouting rocks as evenly spaced as pickets in a fence. Immediately we began to maneuver in the hope of finding an opening. At each end of the shelf were spouts larger than the rest. They seemed like anchoring posts for the fence itself. Back and forth sped the canoes and so intent was I in my search, I failed to notice I had drifted dangerously close to the ledge, so close in fact I was no longer able to escape but would have to shoot through and take a chance, point the bow toward the fence and trust we would clear without touching.

Just as we were both ready to jump into the water, I saw a narrow rift between two spouts, and shot through it without even grazing the rocks. The other canoes found gateways of their own and soon we were down below, laughing rather nervously at what we had done.

No sooner had we headed toward the broad open reaches of Namew than we found that the wind was up and long, uneasy rollers were washing into the river's mouth. For a time we hugged an aspen-covered shore until we could see which side of the lake offered better shelter. As we rounded a low point, to our amazement we were confronted with two tall, brick chimneys rising out of the trees. For a moment we simply sat and stared. We had suddenly been spewed out of the wilds of the Churchill and the Sturgeon Weir into a land of man-made structures. Elliot, I remembered, had mentioned the ruins some days before, had explained the failure of a government educational venture for the Crees, and told us about the eventual burning down of the buildings. It had been the end of a dream to set up a self-sufficient farm school near the mining community of Flin Flon in the hope of helping the Crees make their adjustment to the white man's way of life.

We paddled to a landing below the chimneys and walked up the hillside toward what was left of the old structures. A few cattle still grazed in an open field nearby and though there was smoke coming from a cabin in the distance, no one was around. There was an air of unreality about it all, a farm carved out of the bush, materials flown in or carted down a trail from Flin Flon. For a time it must have been a beehive of activity with high hopes, but now all that was over and the country was reverting to aspen, birch, and spruce saplings. Unless the road was swiftly improved it would not be long before the wilderness would reclaim its own.

We returned to the canoes. After pushing away from the decayed timbers of what had once been a dock, but before heading out into the lake, we looked once more at the chimneys of Namew standing tall and straight and fire-scarred on the river's bank.

Their very presence was a threat to the old wilderness, a threat evidenced by the Dew Line along the Arctic coast and the burgeoning populations to the south. Even now the trails of great wheeled tractors crisscrossed the tundra near the Arctic Sea, tundra that until now had known only the tracks of caribou and men on foot. In a few years there would be no place in the North where men could not go. True, the aurora would still flame and blaze across the skies and husky dogs still howl around the villages, but something would be gone— that intangible sense of remoteness and solitude that comes only from inaccessibility. The river above the chimneys, even with the smoke of Flin Flon in the distance, had seemed part of the old tradition. Except for Stanley and Pelican Rapids there had been no change since the age of discovery.

We pointed the canoes toward the open reaches of Namew. The waves were really rolling now, long smooth swells that moved the weeds and debris in restless windrows. Far out in the open we could see the whitecaps coming directly toward us, but we had no choice if we were to keep to our schedule. We must fight them to the end of the lake, no matter how rough they became. This would be different from running with the wind as we had on Amisk. For fifteen or twenty miles the challenge was clear, for there were no islands or points to use for cover, no protection whatsoever, just wide-open expanses of water. Down the lake toward the outlet was an open horizon—the vast blue mistiness of space. Such a thing we had seen our first day on Ile à la Crosse when we rounded the point at the entrance to the Athabasca Channel. We had found it on Rainy Lake when we faced its forty miles of storm on the way to Fort Francis, for a moment on Amisk, and on the Snake. We knew it one morning on the shore of Lake Superior just before we made the Grand Portage around the rapids of the Pigeon. Each time we saw one it was a thrilling experience, a throwback perhaps to the days when most of the planet was open horizon, and cities, towns, and villages only a thin line along the edge of the wild. Beyond that line was the challenge of the unknown, in the blue distances uncertainty and often fear. When men crossed it, they gambled with fate, and if they returned, they came with strange and wonderful tales.

To modern man there is still the old appeal and I knew as we sat there in our canoes looking out over Namew that in that misty horizon was the difference between merely natural country and the old concept of wilderness. There before us was the sense of the old frontier. Beyond that blue was Cumberland House, an outpost of empire, and we were voyageurs from the far Northwest. As we pushed ahead we forgot about the chimneys of Namew. In that horizon was what we had come to find.

Here was our first real test of fighting our way against the waves. True we had fought them over short distances but this time there was a powerful southwester coming straight down the lake. We had not gone a quarter mile before we knew we must cross to the southern shore and find what little shelter there might be. We started quartering immediately and soon found ourselves riding against enormous rollers with broad intervals between them, intervals wide enough for the canoes to coast down one incline and up the other and be almost hidden from sight in the process. Had it not been for the breadth of the troughs it would have been impossible to make headway. We attempted to pass a low swampy island to the left and for an hour barely held our own. Over and over again we battled to the hissing crests of waves, slipped over their tops, and went tobogganing down with enough momentum to climb the next pinnacle.

Tony was enjoying it immensely, and it was a pleasure to watch the way he adjusted his weight and balance to the pitching of the canoe. It seemed to me that he was doing more than ride a canoe, that something else was going through his mind. No man could go through his somewhat exaggerated motions of shifting weight and very apparent joy of arriving at the top of each wave without drawing on some other experience. As we started down a foaming crest he turned and with a wild light in his eyes, yelled: "Like riding a horse!" Tony, I remembered, had been a polo player. Now the old reactions were his again and he was following the ball across the field, weaving, swaying, wielding his paddle as though it were a mallet in his hands. "See where the other canoes are," I shouted, for it was impossible to look back for even an instant without danger of losing control. He turned but was in the trough and could see nothing. At the peak of the next crest he tried again.

"Omond's down the middle," he yelled, "no sign of Elliot and Eric."

He grabbed his paddle just in time as we shot down the next incline.

No sign of the third canoe. Anything could happen. I turned the first chance I had and finally caught a swift glimpse of the canoe all but disappearing in the waves. They were making progress just like us—slow, tortuous progress of not more than a mile or a mile and a half an hour. We headed for a slight promontory on the left shore several miles beyond. The swampy island, much to our surprise, was now well behind us and we were beginning to feel the shelter of the lee side. After another two hours we reached it, landed and climbed to the highest ledge and waited for Eric and Elliot, gloating in the realization we had made it. They were still pouring into their paddling all the energy and skill they possessed. Far out in the open Omond and Denis were also fighting their way, the canoe a tiny silver speck but making headway toward another promontory two miles beyond ours. At first I wondered why they had chosen what seemed like an unnecessarily difficult and dangerous course until I remembered that Denis had commanded a craft in the North Atlantic during the war, had learned long ago that the smoothest water is far from shore currents and turbulence. His navy experience was now paying off, for they were having easier going than we and would be far ahead of us when they landed. There they could sit and watch us fight toward our rendezvous, even as we watched Eric and Elliot now.

Eric and Elliot soon joined us, and after resting a moment we headed for the point Omond and Denis were now approaching two miles beyond. We saw them land on a protected shelf and an hour later joined them on another flat ledge of limestone similar to the one we had camped on the night before. That noon we had a big pot of tea and what was left of the beans I had cooked at Goose Creek. They tasted good after the workout we had had. Say what you will about cold drinks, there is nothing like a cup of hot tea when the going has been rough. After lunch we stretched out in the sunshine.

A movement down at the water's edge caught my eye, a mink gliding like a snake between the broken bits of ledge. Almost black, the animal would soon be prime, a good pelt for the trade. In the old days it took four of them to equal one beaver in value, but now the story is quite different, for the mink in all its variations in color is one of the most sought-after furs in the market. It has become synonymous with luxury and wealth.

Jonathan Carver in his *Travels through the Interior Parts of North America in the years 1766, 1767, 1768*, though somewhat in error, had this to say of the mink:

"The mink is of the otter kind, and subsists in the same manner. In shape and size it resembles a pole-cat, being equally long and slender. Its skin is blacker than that of an otter, or almost any other creature; 'as black as a mink,' being a proverbial expression in America; it is not however so valuable, though this greatly depends on the season in which it is taken. Its tail is round like that of a snake, but growing flattish toward the end, and is entirely without hair. An agreeable musky scent exhales from its body; and it is met with near the sources of rivers on whose banks it chiefly lives."

The little animal worked its way toward us investigating every cranny, stopped for a tremulous moment within a few feet of where we were resting. Its black beady eyes were steady and venomous, its whiskers twitching.

Someone coughed and moved.

Instantly the sinuous body stiffened, teeth were bared, and from its throat came a chirring hiss. Here was a killer true to

256

form, defying creatures far larger than itself. One of the weasel family, the Mustelidae, the mink was typical of them all. One more glimpse and it was gone, just a flash between the rocks.

I turned then to get a better view and heard a metallic click as something fell down into a crevice beneath me. Gone was all thought of the mink. My knife had slipped out of my pocket, a knife that had a story behind it and certain sentimental value. My son had picked it up in Italy during the war and I hated to lose it. I turned over carefully, shaded my eyes, and caught a tiny glint on a narrow shelf six feet below. I wondered if I could tie a gang hook from one of the fishing baits onto a willow stick and snare it. I took a three-pronged hook, tied it securely to a stick and began to fish, but each time I touched it even lightly it slid a little farther down and at last dropped with a final click twenty feet below on another ledge and completely out of reach.

"Again the Mamaygwessey," said Tony who had been watching me with interest. "Each time they pull it away from you."

After lunch we proceeded down the shore. Flat ledges were everywhere, acres and acres of them, and the one we had first found at Goose Creek was dwarfed in comparison. The wind had shifted directly into the south and it turned very warm, the first real wave of heat we had felt since the expedition began. Leaving Namew we entered a marshy estuary with the shores becoming flatter and flatter, the limestone ledges barely above the high-water mark, grown thickly with willows and bor dered with sedge. Again we wondered if we would have to make camp our last night in some swamp or if we might continue to be lucky and find a site high enough to be away from flies and keep the outfit dry.

There were several promising places across the lake, so Tony and I paddled toward them. Omond and Denis explored a rocky-looking point some distance below us and Elliot and Eric the opposite shore. But the rocks proved only jumbles of scattered and tilted ledges with approaches so shallow the canoes could never land. We paddled to where Omond and Denis were signaling. They had found a fairly good approach, even though the rocks were slippery with moss and algae.

Back of the landing was a level sandy ridge where Indians had camped in the past, and there we strung up the tents for the last time. Because of the heat we needed a swim, but the slippery rocks and the shallows made it impossible to reach deep enough water. We sloshed around in a few inches and gradually crawfished our way out to where we were actually covered.

Swimming had become a tradition with us on all our expeditions, and we usually went in at the slightest provocation, our philosophy being that getting the feel of water was as necessary as cleanliness and the pleasure involved. Like beaver we must never worry about the possibility of getting wet. Running a rapids or fighting a storm such as we had just done could be a frightening experience if there was the constant fear of upsetting. While no one wanted such a thing to happen, being immersed bodily was never of great moment. I have always marveled at the fear of water Indians and experienced woodsmen often have, even though they spend their lives upon it. Now I know it is simply that many of them have never learned to swim, carrying with them the innate fear of death in a strange element. So we bathed even when there was barely enough water to cover us. We became clean, but more important than that, like the beaver, we felt at home.

Here was an ancient camp site with many tent places well back from the water's edge, an abundance of firewood, dry poplar and birch and spruce with plenty of old shredded bark. We lined our tents again with spruce from a fallen tree and for the last time smelled the good clean smell of resin.

That night as we sat eating our supper we heard the drone of an outboard to the south and knew we were close to the trading post at Cumberland House. It was our last camp, our last night out of doors, and there was only one more day to plan for, with seventeen miles to go.

The moon in its third quarter hung pale and yellow over the horizon. By the time it was full we would be on our way home.

CHAPTER 21

CUMBERLAND HOUSE

W*E leave the Saskatchewine by entering the river which forms the discharge of the Sturgeon Lake, on whose east bank is situated Cumberland House. . . . The distance between the entrans and Cumberland House is estimated at twenty miles. It is very evident that the mud which is carried down by the Saskatchewine River, has formed the land that lies between it and the lake, for the distance of upwards of twenty miles in the line of the river which is inundated during one half of the summer, though covered with wood.*

—ALEXANDER MACKENZIE

WITH THE REALIZATION the following morning that we had only seventeen miles to go, the spur for an early start was gone. It was different now from the days when we made over thirty miles between take-off and sundown. This morning we could loaf. It was humid and very warm. The paddle across the shallow marshlands of Cumberland would be slow and tiring.

"Did you hear the thunder last night?" asked Elliot as we got ready for breakfast.

"No," I replied, "didn't hear a thing, and there doesn't seem to be any sign of rain."

"I heard something," he said, "sort of a rolling peal and then a thunderclap, not too far away."

We ate the usual breakfast, Red River cereal and fruit, some bannock, bacon and coffee, packed our bags for the last time, glad that the outfit was dry and ready for shipment to the outside. Wet packs or tents might have mildewed on the long trip ahead. The packs were much lighter, for during the trip food had been distributed in all of them, and now the surplus was gone. The lunch pack held all we would need for the noon snack and supper at Cumberland House.

We worked hard on the cooking outfit, for we might not use the pots again. We scoured them inside and out, polished the outer layer of carbon to the point where the pails really shone. Plates, cups, knives, forks, and spoons were cleaned carefully, sorted, and packed in their containers. The axes were thoroughly wiped, tucked into their sheaths and into the proper corners of the tent packs. There was a certain sadness to all this, caused by our reluctance to cut our last ties with the bush. Finally everything was ready, but it was midmorning before we slid the canoes over the slippery limestone ledges, waded out with them to deeper water, and started down the narrows of Namew.

There were many gulls and terns now and occasional flocks of mallards. We passed through Whitey Narrows and then into Cross Lake. The water had become murky and the shores much swampier than before. We were approaching the muddy waters of the great Saskatchewan, highway to the Northwest and chief reason for the establishment of Cumberland House by Samuel Hearne in 1774. As the first far inland outpost of the Hudson's Bay Company beyond York Factory, it had been a bid for the fur trade of the entire area.

The limestone now disappeared and the shallow lake became a vast weed bed. It was slow and tedious paddling and almost impossible at times. Far ahead, an Indian with a large canoe and motor dodged repeatedly between the weed beds, stopping every few minutes to tilt his motor and clear off its propeller, starting off only to be stalled again. Once he jumped out in a shallow place and pulled his canoe ahead. Many times we were tempted to do the same, for it seemed much easier than paddling.

All morning we pushed from one open spot to another, got caught in heavy weed beds time after time, felt the deadly drag with each paddle stroke, finally gave up and poled. The heat shimmering over the great flats, the swarms of flies, the screaming gulls and terns and the mirage-like visions of clean open water in the distance made progress interminably slow. We knew there would be a welcome at Cumberland House, possibly dinner at the manager's, a chance for a bath and clean clothes. All this we thought about as we dragged our way ahead, but each bed of weeds, every shallows, the smell of muddy water and the heat conspired to postpone such delights.

As we worked our way along, I could not help but think that of all places to pick for the site of a Hudson's Bay Post here was the worst possible choice. With clear deep waterways all the way down the Churchill, why single out a stinking shallow morass for such an important site? We knew the answer, of course, and it had nothing to do with sweating voyageurs, only with the fact that here was a crossroads of the north and an ideal place for trade. Personal convenience or aesthetic considerations were of little importance compared to strategy of location.

David Thompson evidently thought the same, for he stated in his journal:

"On west side of these alluvials is Cumberland Lake on the east bank of which is situated Cumberland House. . . . This House was the first inland trading post the Hudson's Bay Company made, remarkably well situated for the trade of fine Furrs; it serves as a general Depot for all dried Provisions made of the meat and fat of the Bison under the name Pemican, a wholesome, well tasted nutritious food, upon which all persons engaged in the Furr Trade mostly depend for their subsistance during the open season. . . . It is at Cumberland House all the

Pimmican and dried provisions of all kinds procured from the great plains are brought down the Saskatchewan and deposited here and which forms the supplies for the furr Traders going to, and coming from, all the trading Posts; By receiving the turbid waters of the Saskatchewan, it has remarkably fine Sturgeon, a fish that requires such water to be in perfection."

Gradually we moved across the great swamp. Far to the east, buildings took form out of the mirage. It was Cumberland House. We stopped paddling. All day it had seemed nebulous. Though we had found it on the maps, still it did not seem real until that moment. There it was across the broad shallow expanse of the lake, shining in the sunlight exactly as it did in 1774, a welcome to travelers from the great river of the Northwest or a last view to voyageurs heading out.

For one hundred and eighty years it had lain there, and there had always been a few cabins to welcome voyageurs. I felt ashamed of being irritated by the swamp, the weed beds, and the mirages shimmering in the heat. What were a few hours of hard paddling compared to the tremendous adventure of achieving an objective such as this, or Grand Portage after a year of absence, or Montreal after two or three thousand miles of travel, the great triumph of actually seeing a place you have dreamed about for weeks or months or years, plumes of smoke and habitations other than your own?

We stopped for lunch on a muddy point with the water so shallow we could barely get the canoes in far enough to step out without getting mired. Again, swarms of flies and gnats buzzed in the heat. It was too muddy to sit down and we ate standing up. So this, I thought, is the country of the Saskatchewan. We did not tarry, but packed our outfit, headed across the last stretch of the lake, rounded a series of low grassy points, and turned into a long narrow bay. There before us were the wharf and the buildings of the post. We had been expected, and no doubt our slow progress down the lake had been watched for hours. At the dock to meet us were some Indians, and Manager Tom McEwen of the Hudson's Bay Company, Constable Vivian Bradley of the Royal Canadian Mounted Police, and Mr. Oliver Shaw, the agent for the Saskatchewan Government.

We had hardly unloaded when a truck roared up. Mr. McEwen looked over the canoes and spoke to the driver. Without more ado, the canoes were loaded onto the truck and disappeared down the short, dusty road toward the warehouse. Somehow it seemed to me that we should have had time to part with dignity. After all, those canoes meant a lot to us—the one with the ribs broken on Leaf Rapids, Omond and Denis's with the cut they got when pushing through the little Riffle down the Weir, the one that had blown across the lake at Dipper. Those three canoes that had carried us through countless rough waters and over the storms of Amisk, Dead, Namew, the craft we had put away so carefully each night, portaged and loaded countless times, were suddenly gone. We watched them disappear with a sense of loss.

"It was better to end here," said Tony, looking down the little road, "better here than turning them over to someone at Flin Flon. At least they will seem more at home at a Hudson's Bay Post than in some warehouse on the main street of a mining camp."

The manager had merely given them a swift glance. From long experience he knew what they were worth as second-hand canoes. To him it was just another matter of storage or a trade, but to us it was like losing old friends. That truck roaring down the road had robbed us of the freedom to come and go, and we were back where we started, dependent once more on our pocketbooks and credentials.

The Indians were loading our packs into another truck. The pack with the red string tied to it was Eric's, and no one during the entire trip had dared touch it for it always rode close to where he sat. Then there was the one with the broken strap, and the one with the patch. Those packs too had personality and had come to mean something to all of us. We had cursed them on the portages, had come to know all about them—how a certain strap could bite into one's wind, whether one would make a good top load or be better underneath, the basket pack which carried everything for lunch and had always occupied a place of honor. Now they, too, were being tossed into the truck and would be carted over to the guest house reserved for the Honourable Company's officials and visiting guests.

"Can't we sleep outside somewhere," asked Omond almost wistfully, "somewhere close to the fringe of trees and toward the edge of the clearing?"

"No," answered Elliot. "Tonight we sleep in beds."

And so we said good-by to the tents with their smell of

smoke and spruce, good-by to the sleeping bags and the cooking outfit, good-by to all the worn, familiar things we had come to know. We made our last portage over a boardwalk, past the trading post and store, and through an open doorway into the guest house, where there were chairs, a table, beds with springs and snowy sheets. I went to the windows and opened them wide. All of us moved awkwardly and ill at ease.

"Well I'll be damned!" Denis said, then laughed and sat down on the nearest bed, bounced up and down like a little boy. "I'll be damned," he said again.

It seemed terribly close in that little house, even with the windows spread wide. From the front room we could look down the expanse of Cumberland Lake and see the weed flats and the circling gulls, the blue horizon toward Namew and the outlet of the Sturgeon Weir. Hurriedly we sorted our personal gear, cleaned up and shaved and got ourselves ready for the arrival of Mr. and Mrs. McEwen. I went to the store for some fruit juice, came back with a can of orange and one of lemon and, unbelievably, a chunk of ice. Omond in keeping with the gravity of the situation again took charge.

Mr. and Mrs. McEwen arrived at five o'clock, exactly on time to the second. Mrs. McEwen, a precise Scotch lady from Glasgow, had been in the bush for many years, she told us, and had never left it.

"She was watching you with field glasses," chuckled Mr. McEwen. "Saw you fighting those weed beds, but was shocked at the way you looked. 'Better tell those men,' she said to me, 'to put their shirts on before coming to the Post.'"

We laughed, but at the moment shirts seemed stifling and the little room unbearably close. After a discreet half hour they invited us to dinner at six and rose to go.

At exactly six o'clock we sat down at a table covered with a white cloth, gleaming silver and china, fresh meat that had not been tinned or dried, and hot home-made bread. I am afraid we overate, especially of the bread. Mrs. McEwen, watching us, told a story of Father Moraud.

"The Indians dearly loved him," she said, "because of his Christlike devotion to the Crees and their simple way of life. When he first came to the post he told us he would never enter a white man's house again, wanted nothing better than the Crees, that their way of life was good enough for him. But one day when I was baking bread he sniffed the air while passing by, stopped, came to the doorway and stood for a while in deep thought. Then he came inside. That fresh bread was the undoing of Father Moraud." She might well have added all of us, if we did not soon take care.

"Mrs. McEwen," said the manager, "has quite a way with men and that is how it has been, clear from Norway House at the end of Lake Winnipeg through all the posts where we have been stationed."

After dinner we were taken on a tour of the post and the Indian hospital of which everyone was very proud. I broke away from the group early and stole back to my bunk and tried to sleep, but the bed was too soft and the air too close. Finally I dressed, went out of doors and headed for the lake shore. I wanted to smell the water, hear the wash of it and get the old feeling once more. I got there just in time to see an orange moon, almost full, climbing above the horizon. Then the huskies started their weird music, and I lay on a grassy bank and listened.

This was the old North, the feel of the wind from the water, the music of the dogs. This was my farewell to the Churchill River country—not Cumberland House, the new hospital, or talk of the outside. I sat there a long time and listened to the sounds of the great marsh, the rustle of reeds and grasses, the lap of water, the far calling of loons, and finally must have dozed. When I woke, the moon was high and a path of glittering silver lay across the lake.

I had promised Mrs. McEwen I would make pancakes for everyone in the morning. Tomorrow would be a long day: ninety miles down the Saskatchewan to The Pas, the flight to Winnipeg, the final packing of the outfit. I worked my way back across the clearing to the guest house. The rest were sound asleep. A cool breeze was now coming through the open windows.

Tony stirred. "Where have you been, Bourgeois?"

"I went to the lake," I said.

"You should have taken me with you," he muttered reproachfully and then was asleep once more.

I was at the McEwens' house a few minutes before five. Mrs. McEwen had a fire crackling merrily in the stove, the big griddle was piping hot and bacon already started. She gave me a huge bowl, flour, fresh eggs, baking powder and salt and I went to work. By the time the voyageurs arrived, cakes were coming off the griddle ten at a time. Mounds of them disappeared, washed down with many cups of coffee. It was a lark for us, and once during the height of the banter while the cakes were rolling from the griddle, she said slyly to me: "Aren't we having fun?" I agreed wholeheartedly. This was fun: pancakes for the first time on the trip. The voyageurs must have eaten a dozen each.

After breakfast we took a two-mile truck ride to Pemmican Portage and loaded our outfit into two waiting motor-driven canoes for the five-hour trip down the river to The Pas. We waved to the Indians who had gathered to see us off and then were in the grip of the brown current, with the motors going full blast. What a great, slow-moving marshy river it was, with low muddy banks and boggy shores. What a contrast to the beautiful country of the Shield. Famous moose and duck hunting to be sure, but the cleanness and charm of the hard high country was not there. I could not help thinking of voyageurs' brigades forcing their way up that river day after day against that slow and powerful current, camps at night on muddy banks, mile after mile of tracking through slippery mud, monotony and more monotony for weeks at a time. After our brief experience on Cumberland Lake and the lower reaches of Namew, this part of the country had little appeal. True, it was pleasant sitting comfortably ensconced on our packs, watching the brushy shores slip by without having to lift a finger, knowing we were making possibly fifteen or twenty miles an hour and doing in a few short hours what would have taken us two days of steady paddling, but I knew this was no country for us.

At noon we were met by Ben Grimmelt of Flin Flon, a mining man whom Denis knew, Bill Chapman of the Royal Bank of Canada, newsmen and photographers—one of them from the *Toronto Star* had flown to meet us and get a story. They asked us many questions.

Why did we make the trip? Why hadn't we taken guides and motors? Did we have any adventures? Had we taken lots of fish, and how about our prospecting for uranium? What did we plan for next year, and would these expeditions go on and on, or was this the last?

We tried to satisfy them all but somehow our answers sounded flat and innocuous. There was really nothing we had done that was exciting or that would make a good story, no hairbreadth escapes or great dangers, nothing but a daily succession of adventures of the spirit, the sort of thing that could not make headlines. Our newspaper friends, I know, were disappointed. They had expected something sensational, but nothing we gave them sounded good.

We had lunch at a hot, busy little restaurant and it was there we saw our first newspaper with the headline, PLANE CRASHES NEAR NAMEW.

"That was your thunderclap," I said to Elliot. "That's what you heard last night on Namew."

Mid-afternoon found us at the airport boarding a plane for Winnipeg. I was lucky enough to get a window seat, where I sat with my face glued to the pane, marveling at the tangled waterways and the marshy rivers down below. Then we were out of the low country and flying over wide prairies and farm-houses and the geometrical symmetry of fields and roads. Ahead in the rosy dusk were the sparkling lights of Winnipeg. The moon, I remembered, should be full. As we came in for a landing, there it was, riding the left wing, the same moon that shone on Namew and over Cumberland a few hundred miles away.

The airport was crowded and noisy, our good-bys very gay and final, and then we were on our way back to the lives we had left. By the time I reached home the whole expedition had begun to seem a little unreal. I spread the equipment out in the yard to give it a final airing before putting it away. There was Eric's pack with the red string, the old basket pack for lunches, and the grate Denis had struggled with on every camp site. I laid out the beaten-up cooking outfit, the blackened pails, the dented plates and cups, hung up the tent that Tony and I had shared, the ponchos, and my sleeping bag.

As I worked over the outfit, the Churchill River seemed far away, and the rapids of the Drum, the Leaf, and the Sturgeon Weir and the great storms on Dead and Amisk only a soft rush-ing in the dusk. I knew it would soon be hard even to imagine the music of huskies around the Indian villages or the wild call-ing of the loons on the open lakes.

I also knew there were some things that would never be dimmed by distance or time, compounded of values that would not be forgotten: the joy and challenge of the wilderness, the sense of being part of the country and of an era that was gone, the freedom we had known, silence, timelessness, beauty, companionship and loyalty, and the feeling of fullness and completion that was ours at the end.

I repacked the outfit and placed each item carefully away. It would not rest too long. Sooner or later it would all come out again. The Reindeer country was waiting: Athabasca, Great Slave, Great Bear, and the vast barren lands beyond them all. Another year perhaps and the Lonely Land would claim us once again.

Known honorifically as The Bourgeois—as *voyageurs* of old called their trusted leaders—by the generation of outdoorsmen he has guided in the wilderness, Sigurd F. Olson is perhaps our country's most famous living woodsman. Born in Chicago in 1899, educated at the University of Wisconsin (Geology) and the University of Illinois (Animal and Plant Ecology), he was professor and dean before abandoning the academy for the wilderness. Mr. Olson is a former President of the National Parks Association; presently member of boards or councils of The Wilderness Society, Isaak Walton League of America, and the White Water Association; and is a consultant to the President's Quetico-Superior Wilderness Committee. He lives in Ely, Minnesota.

January 1961

A NOTE ON THE TYPE

The text of this book was set on the Linotype in Janson, a recutting made direct from the type cast from matrices long thought to have been made by Anton Janson, a Dutchman who was a practicing type-founder in Leipzig during the years 1668–87. However, it has been conclusively demonstrated that these types are actually the work of Nicholas Kis (1650–1702), a Hungarian who learned his trade most probably from the master Dutch type-founder Dirk Voskens.

Composed, printed, and bound by
Kingsport Press, Inc., Kingsport, Tenn.
Paper manufactured by
P. H. Glatfelter Co., Spring Grove, Pa.
Binding based on designs by
CHARLES E. SKAGGS